BULLETPROOF YOUR MINDSET

THINK LIKE A BUSINESS OWNER

PAUL CAMPBELL AUCOIN

PREFACE

Taking personal responsibility has transformed my life. No other idea has come close. - Paul Campbell Aucoin.

I hung up the phone with my lawyer, who confirmed I had sold the company. It was official.

I sat back in my chair, looking around my office. Soon, none of this would matter. The company I started in the basement of my town house sixteen years earlier no longer belonged to me. Two weeks from now, someone else would sit in this chair. I was pretty sure I wouldn't miss it. We had a great run, but the last few years had been really tough.

The sale would allow me to retire. The financial windfall was always in the back of my mind, as one of the key reasons I started my own business. I was nervous, excited, giddy, and sad. I was all over the place.

The hard work, the long hours, and the stress would all translate into a significant tax-exempt payout, also known as a capital gains exemption. Never has an accounting term sounded so sweet.

PREFACE

A few days later, as it all sank in, I reflected on my career and the wild ride I had been on. There had been some exceptional highlights and some brutal lowlights. Staying positive was a regular challenge.

I found getting better every day helped me feel I was in control of my life. Constant improvement resonated with me so strongly, I made it a core value of our company. I wanted others to experience that same sense of control.

I worked on conflict resolution, running effective meetings, implementing processes into an organization, negotiating skills, understanding personality styles, emotional intelligence, time management, and public speaking.

I was a member of a business owner, peer advisory group, for the last fourteen years. In that group were some of the smartest, most profitable industry leaders in our business community. I received amazing advice from them. I would miss our spirited exchanges.

But, my number one differentiator, was taking personal responsibility whenever I could. It had been with me since I was twenty-five years old. It created a path to understanding. It turned emotional conflicts into manageable compromises. It helped me solve problems with integrity.

I've always wanted to explain my interpretation in a short sound bite. But I haven't been able to.

For instance, if I asked you to, "Take responsibility", you'll likely respond, "I think I do that already. But it's not fun."

When pressed, you might say that the essence of responsibility falls in statements like these:

- Do what you're supposed to do.
- Do your job.
- Do your chores.
- Be on time.

PREFACE

None of that sounds fun. But that's not it. That's the boring side of taking responsibility. You need to dig deeper. It gets fun when you dig deeper.

I had been through some messy situations where I did not want to take responsibility. The toughest ones were when I had three avenues I could choose, and none of them were good. I remember having butterflies in my stomach the size of pterodactyls as I tried to decide which bitter pill I would swallow.

I learned to push my way through these situations. I would not let these circumstances define me. I was in charge, always. And I could achieve anything I believed I could. Setbacks were just part of the process and actually strengthened me.

I learned to take responsibility bit by bit and turned it into a habit. When I had a tough issue to solve, I would ask myself if I could control any aspect of this issue. Could I take responsibility in some small way?

In the beginning, I was certain there were situations where I had no control. But I found there was always something I could do. And the more I learned about people, and myself, ahh..., the more control I had.

Early on, I learned to appreciate the differences of other people through personality styles. I studied generational values. I dove into books on introversion and extroversion. I read biographies.

I wouldn't give up because someone acted irrationally. I wouldn't say, "What is wrong with that person?", and walk away, feeling offended.

Taking responsibility instilled a core value that shaped who I am. My conundrum has been explaining it so it's useful for others. I believe I have done that here.

Join me on a short journey on how to Bulletproof your Mindset, and dig deeper to discover how to take more control of your life.

INTRODUCTION

"I know you believe you understand what you think I said, but I am not sure that you realize that what you heard is not what I meant."
Robert McCloskey, U.S. State Department spokesperson (1964-1974)

Communication is a critical skill we use every day, yet we rarely make an effort to improve it.

Every day we have opportunities to change our outcome based on how we communicate. We can choose to be positive, and we can choose to be friendly. We can choose to smile and say hello to a stranger we pass on the street.

The vast majority don't consider regular communication as a skill. We agree that sales, negotiating and public speaking are skills, but not our regular interactions.

The incoming president of our local industry association gave a ten-minute speech without notes and was given a warm ovation from the crowd of two hundred engineers and contractors. He presented a simple message, sprinkled some self-deprecating humor, and left us laughing. I leaned over to my colleague and

INTRODUCTION

commented on how well prepared the speech was. My friend didn't think he prepared. He was a natural. I decided to find out.

I made my way to the front of the room and waited for the well-wishers to thank the speaker. I introduced myself and thanked him for an excellent speech and asked whether he was a Toastmaster. He studied me and smiled. "I am a Toastmaster! What gave me away?"

"Well, your speech was excellent. It had a great opening, body and conclusion: no notes, excellent humor and natural gestures. As a fellow Toastmaster, I know how much practice goes into such a well-planned speech. Don't worry, everyone else thinks you're a natural." I smiled.

When we see great communication, we chalk it up to someone being gifted, whether it's naturally funny, smart, confident, or charismatic. Ask a "gifted" person, or talented comedian, and they will confirm it's a result of hard work. They work at their communication, and it comes across naturally.

Experienced speakers like these are so well prepared that if we interrupt them, they can comment about the interruption, laugh about it, and continue where they left off, without missing a beat.

There are thousands of books on various forms of communication. There are night classes and organizations that teach public speaking, sales and negotiating. People attend one course, one time and consider themselves a trained communicator or public speaker.

It's a waste if that's where it ends. There is so much more for us to discover.

Improving one's communication doesn't need to start with public speaking or negotiating. Many people believe they will never use these skills, so why bother?

INTRODUCTION

My greatest improvement in communication skills came by taking personal responsibility for more aspects of my life. Those communication skills dwarfed those I learned in public speaking training.

Taking responsibility began with three steps:

1. Self-affirm that taking more control of your life is possible in every situation.
2. Acknowledge when your mindset is agitated or frustrated. Increase your self-awareness and, along with it, your emotional intelligence.
3. Take control of your mindset. Act now and take control.

Using these steps as a foundation, I needed a shortcut or habit to remember those steps.

I overcame step one, which took some time. I was certain I couldn't take control in many situations. I expect many others will struggle with this one as well. By the time you get to Chapter seven, your perspective should change.

Eventually I could control any situation in some small way, so I didn't need to repeat that step. Then I experimented with an idea to incorporate the other steps.

I modified step two to include catching myself being frustrated, agitated, complaining, angry, or blaming.

Step three was to take control.

I came up with ABC. Pretty original, right! A for Angry, B for Blame, and C for taking Control. That seemed memorable. I tried it out the following week, and it seemed to work. When I found myself angry or blaming, I needed to take more control, even if the only way was to control my mindset.

After a few weeks, I added the word Intent to the acronym, because it was consistently the best first strategy for taking control. So, I made it ABCI. Then I recognized ABC1, number 1, was easier to remember. So, I use ABC1. Anger Blame Control Intent. I still use that shortcut as my first strategy.

Now that I had a reliable method to use, I was taken aback at how often I was agitated. Prior to this, I had considered myself an extremely optimistic, positive person. But all these little issues were bubbling below the surface. I was suppressing them.

As I expanded ABC1 to more complex issues, I noticed Intent didn't always help me take control. I dug deeper over the next several years and found concepts that broadened my ability to remain in control of my mindset. They include:

- Understanding personality styles such as DISC.
- Understanding how our brain reacts when we are upset and losing control, which is connected to Emotional Intelligence.
- The impact of friends and family on our mindset.
- How to set goals that strengthen our self-worth.
- Coming to grips with our baseline skills, our good, our bad and our ugly.

This book isn't just for businesspeople. Many of my examples come from the business world, but the principles relate to all aspects of our lives. And to bulletproof your mindset, you will need to have a handle on your personal life. Your mindset takes all your experiences into account, and if your personal life is in shambles, it will ultimately affect your business life, and vice versa.

How you respond to your challenges will define not just your business, but yourself. While there will be many surprises, you can prepare your mindset to welcome change and challenges.

INTRODUCTION

Opportunities hide within obstacles if you're open to discover them. This is the growth mindset, and it's a key component to building a successful life.

This resourcefulness is common in business owners who adopt some vulnerability. Those who admit they don't know it all. They are humble. They have embraced the concept: you don't know what you don't know. It keeps their mind open to new ideas and new technologies.

Join me in this journey where you will learn about yourself, a typical business owner, and the people around you. Each step along the way will broaden your ability to bulletproof your mindset.

As you practice these skills, you will notice how difficult it becomes for you to feel offended. You can maintain your composure in the most intense situations. You see beyond their mask and allow them to see beyond yours. Your confidence is obvious. People trust you because they can sense your positive intent.

Your communication skill is unrivaled.

THE ENTREPRENEUR MINDSET

"*Success is a little like wrestling a gorilla. You don't quit when you're tired; you quit when the gorilla is tired.*"
Robert Strauss, US Ambassador to Soviet Union.

I HAVE MET hundreds of business owners and provided counsel for over a hundred of them. At some point in a successful business owner's evolution, they decide to take complete control of their destiny. They take on the gorilla. What happens next differentiates the successful from the average.

The successful business owner finds valuable time by getting up early, working late, or working on the weekends. They know their dream will take time and perseverance, but it will be worth it. They take calculated risks. They take on any challenge, be it legal, finance, sales, IT, or operations. They solve issues themselves or find the right person who can help them solve it. They push through their daily struggle using their strong, positive mindset.

When this owner experiences a setback, they remain positive. Instead of blaming others, they accept the outcome and establish a process so it won't re-occur. They don't blame customers, suppliers, or employees for mistakes. They take responsibility and use it as fuel to solve those mistakes.

I tried sharing my similar observations with others. If a colleague was blaming a circumstance, and I suggested they take responsibility... I would invariably hit a nerve. If I got a response, it would be: "There's nothing I can do about that", or "It's someone else's fault", or my favorite, "Whatever!" They didn't want a discussion. They wanted me to stop insinuating it was their fault.

Whatever I had learned didn't communicate well with others.

I decided others would eventually learn about taking responsibility. I was ahead of the curve. They would learn it soon enough. I stopped talking about it.

The blaming never stopped, though. It was everywhere.

> Successful small business owners didn't talk that way. Blaming outside circumstances never entered their minds. They reveled in these types of challenges. It didn't matter if they didn't understand a business situation, they would figure it out or find someone that could.

IAN IS a successful and well-respected business leader in his community, and was my first boss. He has a beautiful home on a lake, a fantastic wife, and two brilliant children. He was past president of our local Board of Trade, a director of our industry group, and admired by his peers.

He had a desk name plate that said, "The buck stops here." It was a light-hearted reminder that he was the boss–big decisions were his to make. What I wouldn't grasp until years later was this was <u>his</u> mantra for taking responsibility. When people were around, he might joke about the name plate, enjoying the power he held. But after everyone went home, that name plate took on a less pleasant significance, that he and every successful business owner experience.

With their head in their hands, late at night, they agonize over a decision they alone need to make. Advice has been sought, files reviewed, and all sides of the story have been considered. The buck stops with them. It's time to decide and take full responsibility for that decision.

For example, their single parent employee needs to be disciplined or fired; a good customer needs to be informed their time-critical equipment will arrive two weeks later than promised; or their business needs a second mortgage to cover a cash flow shortfall. It's gut-check time, and it's on them.

I DEFINE this business owner as one with an Entrepreneurial Mindset, who we'll call EM.

Let's use an example.

Imagine a receptionist informs their business owner a client has offended them. If the owner is focused on who caused the offense, they might call the client and explain how they had upset their receptionist.

The client responds it was the receptionist who was acting sensitive and places the blame on the receptionist. The owner is unprepared for the angry client and responds with an apology and a promise to look into from their end. The situation has got worse instead of better. They have an upset client and are questioning the integrity of their receptionist.

On the other hand, the EM owner approaches the same issue

from a taking responsibility perspective. Their strategy differs from the beginning.

Step one is for the EM to remain in control of the situation, where it would be easy to become emotional. We will assume the EM's goal is to maintain good relations with both the client and the receptionist.

Step two is to not blame anyone. Easier said than done.

Step three is to take control and assume positive intent for all parties.

In summary, we are using ABC1. Anger, Blame, Control, Intent.

Despite there being no obvious urgency to solve the issue, time is of the essence. Memories fade. A person's interpretation of an emotional event solidifies to match their version of events. If someone is going to apologize, it must happen before the person shares their modified memory with friends and colleagues, the version where they are the victim, and everyone else is the bad guy.

The EM would meet with the receptionist and ask for a full accounting of the story. If there is a Human Resources person in the firm, they would also attend that meeting. The goal is to show support for the receptionist, understand the full story, and hypothesize what the client's reaction might be.

Will the client blame the receptionist? Is it possible the client had positive intent and never intended to offend them? What if they did not know they were even offended?

The EM may ask for background from others in the office who know the client. Has this happened before?

This may seem like too much work, for a seemingly minor problem. But it's not a minor problem, especially for your receptionist, and especially if the receptionist has never brought something like this to you before. It is a big deal for them. If you value your receptionist, you will make it a big deal for you.

Next, is to plan the conversation with the client. The EM

will use a tone of openness, and wanting to understand, rather than being judgmental. The EM would make it clear that their clients are very important to them, and so are their staff. It may have been a misunderstanding, or people being frustrated with each other, which happens. Emphasizing that there was positive intent on both sides, will allow both sides to admit they it may just have been a big misunderstanding.

The client could react in multiple ways. They may offer an apology for being overly expressive in the moment or perhaps didn't realize they said anything offensive. Or, they may have entrenched their view of the event, and are listening to see if they are being blamed. Most importantly, they will react to the EM's tone. That will set the stage for the conversation.

Where there is no repeat offender and the offense is not serious, making one person wrong solves nothing. The best resolution is where the receptionist (accuser) feels heard and respected, and the client (defendant) feels heard and given the benefit of the doubt. They both know, however, that a similar event will not be taken lightly. The EM's integrity has grown in both parties' eyes, for taking on a testy situation head-on.

This is hard work. Blaming is way easier. To solve it properly requires more brain power than you might want to give. It's uncomfortable. It's unclear how it will unfold. But the result is well worth it.

I had a similar example happen to me, and the appreciation it brought me from my receptionist blew me away. She was so happy I had listened to her, stood by her side, and had a tough conversation with an important client to ensure it didn't happen again. I could tell she was nervous when she brought the incident to me. In my mind, I had no choice. I had to take responsibility. I had to take control. I could not blame.

. . .

So how do you develop this Entrepreneurial Mindset? How do you practice being a business owner? How do you practice firing someone who will be traumatized if they lose their job? How do you practice losing a sale you need to pay this month's rent? What happens if a new competitor enters your market and pursues your best customers? What if your number one customer declares bankruptcy while owing you a ton of money?

Are you able to handle the risks that go with owning your business? Has your life partner bought in one hundred percent, both financially and emotionally? Can you disaster-proof yourself and your business?

The typical reply is, I'll figure it out when I get to that point. It doesn't apply to me. Plus, there's nothing I can do right now.

Not correct. There is always something you can do. And you can do it right now.

"You cannot connect the dots looking forward, you can only connect them looking backwards. So you have to trust that the dots will somehow connect in your future." Steve Jobs.

You need to look forward and create your dots for your future. You need to plan with intention. Your dots may not connect right away, but the more strategic dots you create, the more likely they will connect when you most need them.

Which dots do I work on?

A skill which connects many dots is preparing to handle a crisis. Handling a crisis is taking responsibility for big problems. Depending on the level of risk you are taking on, you will face a crisis of equal proportion. The bigger the risk, the better prepared for crisis management you must be.

It is very common to say, my business is not that complicated. I won't experience any crisis I can't deal with.

Delay this preparation at your peril.

Instead, you can prepare now and enjoy doing it.

If you aren't running a business, you will still need advisers. Get to know people in different fields, the skills they have, and how they might help you one day. Knowing you have this team on standby will give you the confidence to pursue more risky, complicated, and lucrative opportunities. You can also share how you could help them one day.

HERE ARE five actions to take:

1. List your business limitations and be brutally honest. What crisis will you need help with?
2. Start networking and asking for contacts that you will need one day. People love to refer others. It makes the business world go around. Can you write someone an online review?
3. When your crisis arrives, you can remind your contact how you already know each other. It's like you are old friends, and you are calling for a small favor.
4. Refer your contacts to your friends. Keep the cycle going.
5. Hire someone. Even if you can do something, someone else can do it cheaper than you. Especially when you compare your lost opportunity cost.

* * *

Lost Opportunity Cost

If you can hire someone to do a task for you, that allows you to earn more than you pay that person, you must do it.

For example, if you spend time bookkeeping for your company, you could hire a remote, part-time bookkeeper. Establish some processes with the bookkeeper and have them produce regular reports you need to stay on top of your financials. This will free you up to do what you do best.

Many of us don't delegate because it places pressure on us to produce. The cost to hire a bookkeeper is predictable. The ability to use that time effectively enough to pay for that cost is how you grow to the next level.

Or you can be one of those owners who doesn't delegate and complain about working too many hours.

Don't forget that lost opportunity cost can include time off. What is vacation time worth to you? If you could free up two hours per week, and you could bank that time, you could book two more weeks' vacation per year.

BEGIN WITH TIP #1—to understand your limitations. We explore this in the "Establishing your baseline" chapter and is key to Bulletproofing your Mindset. Note areas you are weak and plan to get help in those areas.

Having a team of experts on your side provides a sense of stability. Without them, the business world can be intimidating. With them, you can remain in control.

TAKEAWAYS:

- A successful entrepreneur takes responsibility and won't blame others.

- Anger, Blame, Control, Intent. ABC1. This is the first step to Bulletproof your Mindset.
- It is much easier to blame than to take control. Don't take the easy path.
- The entrepreneur grows their business by delegating tasks to maximize their opportunity cost.
- The successful entrepreneur assembles an advisory team well ahead of a crisis.

TAKE RESPONSIBILITY

"The price of greatness is responsibility." Winston Churchill.

I HAD MOVED TO HALIFAX, Nova Scotia, Canada, two years previously. My new friends opened my eyes to the world of personal development books. As an ambitious twenty-five-year-old sales engineer, I poured through their recommended books and audiobooks, lapping up this hidden wealth of information.

I usually found one great concept in each book, and then tried to develop a simple habit that made it easier to remember to use the knowledge I learned. A few special authors were fantastic speakers, which made it easier to drive home their ideas. I listened to them on repeat in my car for weeks at a time.

ONE DAY, I came across the concept of taking responsibility and struggled with what it prescribed. There were some good ideas, but others seemed flat-out nonsensical. I kept thinking about those ideas and wondered, What if they were right? What if, by blaming others, I was actually giving them control of my problems? That didn't seem right. Was it possible I had more control over my career than I thought?

I WAS certain my boss had one hundred percent control of my career!

I NEARLY ABANDONED THE EXERCISE, but something made me stick with it. I forced myself to think of a situation where I was blaming. OK. That part was easy. I was blaming my boss, Ian.

Ian was a good guy, but he frustrated me. He was the owner and lead sales engineer for our top clients. He left me to toil away with the entry-level clients, fighting for every small project. I told Ian I would love to handle one of his clients, but he would sidestep any conversation about it.

The second issue was Ian had promised he would send me to a business finance course–the same one he had attended ten years earlier and raved about. I reminded him I was eager to go on that course, but I could sense he was reconsidering. This perk he had half-promised was evaporating. Maddening.

I was clearly the victim of Ian's lack of consideration. He was in control, and he could do whatever he wanted while I waited. Couldn't he at least give me a plan? How about some timing on when I would get a larger client? Three months? Six months? And that finance course... that sounded really interesting. Was he going to send me or not?

OK. So I can take control of this somehow?

. . .

TAKING responsibility encouraged me to listen to my self-talk and be conscious of what I was feeding my brain. I thought my self-talk was positive, but with Ian..., I sounded weak. My words had a victim mentality to them. I was blaming him. I could feel my stomach turn. I did not like having the word 'victim' associated with me.

As I poured over the issue in my head, I forced myself to consider Ian's point of view. He wasn't doing any of this maliciously. In fact, he had been a great boss to this point. He cared about my future. As nice as he was, though, he was infuriating me.

Without realizing it, I took those first three steps I had learned on taking responsibility.

- Number one, I wanted to be in control so I could stop feeling like a victim.
- Number two, I was frustrated with small-time clients and not attending the finance course. Part of that frustration was with Ian, but more with the situation than with him.
- Step three was to regain control of my positive, healthy mindset. That would prove to be a little tricky.

HOW COULD I take control of these situations?
I racked my brain until I finally had an epiphany.

IAN DID NOT HAVE ill intent toward me. In fact, he had an overall positive intent toward my progress. He was not trying to upset me. But he was. But he didn't mean to. But it still made me upset with him.

Aha... That was a critical distinction. I needed to judge Ian with his intention, not my interpretation of his intention.

"WE JUDGE ourselves by our intentions and others by their behavior." Stephen M.R. Covey, Seven Habits of Highly Successful People.

I DECIDED I needed to judge Ian the way I judged myself. I needed to start with assuming positive intent. If I assumed positive intent, I could tamp down my frustration and regain control of my mindset. Being angry didn't allow me to be creative. (We deal with how to handle negative intent in a future chapter.)

Now that I reasoned Ian had positive intent, I was no longer upset with him. I didn't need to fight him; I needed to reason with him. I needed to help him understand how my recommendations were best for him and his business. I needed to be strategic and clear with my message. I could leave nothing open for interpretation. That's how I got into this situation in the first place.

I made an appointment with Ian.

Don't drop in on your boss when it's a critical conversation.
When you want your boss to know you're serious, don't just drop in to talk. Make an appointment for ten minutes. Even if their office is directly beside you and is always open to you dropping in.

First, it's rare for anyone to refuse a ten-minute meeting. Second, the other person will know you have a focused topic you want to discuss, and they will focus as well.

This is a big deal. Just don't overstay your ten minutes, or you might not get a second meeting.

Ian and I sat down for ten minutes.

I made a case to take over one specific client. Ian had secured very little of this client's business over the last few years. They were next door to one of my clients, and I was on an industry committee with their estimator. I asked for permission to drop in on his client and leave some brochures behind when I was nearby. This would allow me to build some rapport and transition smoothly if Ian transferred the client to me.

In the meantime, I stated, I would remain positive, not complain, and do the best I could with the clients I had. I respected it was his company and his decision. I would demonstrate I was worthy of a top client, and everyone would benefit from the switch.

At the end of our short meeting, I was satisfied I had done all I could; I had been crystal clear with my messaging, and I had a plan.

I overcame the first hurdle. Ian allowed me to drop in on his client.

One month later, I asked Ian how else I could prepare myself. He offered me some good advice and seemed to be warming up to the idea.

Meanwhile, I purchased a remote learning course on finance for a hundred and fifty dollars. I was tempted to keep Ian in the dark on this, but I reminded myself of Ian's positive intent. I shared what I had bought, and he was very pleased I was taking this important step to understand how a business operates.

As I thought about his intent on sending me to that course, I realized it was probably too early in my career to benefit from the advanced course he had attended. Doing so might send me a signal he wanted me to buy his business, which I knew was many years down the road. That was likely why he had been so elusive.

> When we don't take responsibility, and we blame, we pigeonhole our thinking. We wonder what evil thoughts are in the other person's mind, when, the great majority of the time, there is no malicious intent.

WITHIN A FEW MONTHS, the strategic spotlight I had cast on Ian's client made it obvious he wasn't paying enough attention to them. He promised to turn them over to me. Woo-hoo!

I expressed my gratitude and promised to keep him in the loop with the client for a few months. I would do him proud.

Wow, did that ever feel good! I went from angry, blaming and out of control, to taking over a client I never thought I would have. Win-win. It took time and perseverance. Valuable wins usually do.

Engineer geek-out.
I'm a fan of acronyms, shortcuts and formulae. I'm an engineer. I can't help it.
When I think of Anger and Blame, and how closely related they are, I conclude that A = B. As one intensifies, so does the other. C is Control and completes the equa-

tion: A x B x C = 1, also known as ABC1. 1 is the constant in the equation. As anger or blame increase, control decreases by the square, in order to equal 1. The more control you have, the less blame or anger you will have.

* * *

TAKEAWAYS

- There is an abundance of great advice in personal development books and audiobooks.
- Taking responsibility is a core skill that will compliment your communication ability
- When you are angry, you are almost always blaming.
- When you blame, you give away control of the situation.
- When you are upset, first assume the other person has positive intent and you might have misunderstood the situation.
- Anger x Blame x Control = 1. Reduce your Blame, and you increase your Control of the situation.

ACT SELF EMPLOYED

"*You are self-employed. You work to pay your bills, build your dreams and create your life, regardless of who signs your paycheck.*" Rob Liano, author of Counter-Attack.

I EXPECTED my first career employer to take care of me. I expected a raise or promotion every other year; I expected them to provide training. I expected paid sick leave. I expected to earn an extra week of vacation every five years. And, of course, they must deposit my paycheck to my account precisely on time, every two weeks.

And yet, I felt like my employer was holding all the cards.

Don't forget, you chose to work for your employer. You sought them out, listened to their terms, and chose to accept their offer. You were probably pretty happy that day. Your financial situation had stabilized, and your career was heading in the right direction.

The other great freedom you have is you can quit! Whenever you want. It's up to you. What?

. . .

So why doesn't that feel like freedom?

Well, where would you go if you left your current job? If this question makes you nervous, take stock of what you bring to the table, and how easy you are to replace. If you are coasting, just punching a clock, that should worry you. If you sit around not being very busy, feeling undervalued, well, you aren't very valuable, are you? You are probably replaceable and maybe overpaid. That's not a good combination.

"You can't be brave if you're tapping out of hard conversations about painful, hard topics. That's what it means to lead." Brene Brown.

Once I understood the concept of taking responsibility for my career, I knew I had to become the master of my career. I couldn't leave anything to chance, including getting fired for pissing my boss off one day. Once this sunk in, I was nervous. I had been a bit of jerk, and my boss could be ruthless. He had fired my sales engineer predecessor after only eight months. He could fire me, too. Then what?

I could not tap out of this painful conversation with myself. I needed to improve now.

It wasn't up to my boss to train me further. I knew I had to ramp up my skills on my own. I kept a low profile over the next few months while I at least got going. This dose of reality had me feeling quite vulnerable.

Many workplaces don't offer opportunities to improve. They don't provide regular training and there is little room for advancement. You get stuck believing you have no control. It is easy to feel trapped.

I was pleasantly surprised that I could find areas to improve that cost nothing. I mixed technical reading, sales skills and business ownership skills into my workday. I took our service manager, Ed, out for coffee once per week, asking him to share some technical issues he had encountered in his career. He loved sharing his war stories and having a young whippersnapper lapping up every word.

MY BOSS SUGGESTED I read through the price catalog. I thought he was kidding. Read the price catalog? Do I read the phone book next? I bit my tongue and opened the price book. Sure enough, the footnotes contained valuable information hidden in plain sight. It definitely took perseverance, but I made my way through that entire book, and became the office expert on pricing nuances.

Hey! I was becoming a little more valuable! And I was doing it through my initiative. That felt good.

I KNOW it is difficult for young adults to envision their career destiny. A common stance to take is "I'm too good for this job." You complain, punch the clock, collect a paycheck, and belittle anyone that thinks they have a future. The mistake is believing no one is noticing your contempt for their workplace. People notice. The boss notices. Your customers notice. But the biggest error is you drive that negative thinking into your mindset.

YOU CREATE your reputation through your actions, whether or not you want to. You create it every day. If you want to change, do it constructively. If you realize this job is not for you, then work quietly to prepare yourself for your next adventure. Don't tear down others to build yourself up.

If you complain, blame, and are uninterested, that becomes your reputation. As you attempt to distance yourself by complaining and degrading your workplace, you reinforce yourself as a victim. If you are complaining now, you'll likely be complaining six months after starting your dream job.

* * *

It's all about our wage, isn't it?

Early in our career, we are so focused on our wage. If there is a difference of one dollar per hour, we will take the job that pays more, with little consideration to the future pay of that career.

Between the prime earning years of forty and sixty years old, the average person will earn two-and-a-half times more than at twenty-five. The best opportunities start modestly, and with dedication provide rewards beyond your expectations.

Most trade business owners were once apprentices. The majority had no inkling they could own their own business. It was the furthest thing from their minds. They worked hard and did their best to impress their boss and the company's clients. Over time, they understood how the business worked and were interested in having their own clients one day. They either worked their way up in one firm, or started up a competing business once they had more experience.

"OPPORTUNITY IS MISSED by most people because it is dressed in overalls and looks like work." *Thomas Edison.*

. . .

DETERMINE the future of your career. You are setting the stage today for what you will ultimately earn. There are opportunities for significant earnings increase over the long haul. Ask prospective employers how much you could make in five, ten, twenty years. If your employer can't share a compelling vision, it's best to know now. An employer with vision and opportunity wants to hire the best and brightest. They have a future planned for their employees.

* * *

ARE there opportunities in all occupations?
My summer sport is golf. Employees who work in a golf shop, or as wait staff in the restaurant, typically earn minimum wage. The golf courses have a difficult time hiring new qualified staff, as they offer little opportunity for advancement.

TERRY WORKED in the pro shop and had an easy way about him. He interacted with the membership, making friends along the way. Three years later, he had an excellent career in sales, in an industry he knew nothing about. A business owner member had a good feeling he could grasp the technical basics of electric motors and hired him as a junior salesperson.

Terry became a District Sales manager ten years later, with six branches reporting to him.

From minimum wage to a distinguished career. Sounds lucky, right? Right place, right time? Then why does the golf course have trouble hiring people? It is clearly a great place to meet people who can hire you.

OPPORTUNITIES HIDE IN SOME CAREERS. You may not understand the industry well enough to know whether an entry level position can lead to greater responsibilities. Don't be discouraged to begin at a lower wage than you are earning now if the future potential looks bright.

In my peer-advisory owner group, I was amazed to see just how many ways there were to own a company and make fantastic money. Some occupations require a lot of schooling, but even more do not. So many of them you would start as an apprentice, green as grass, and grow into the owner of a company. The opportunities are all around.

How do you find these golden nuggets?

You cannot hit a target you cannot see. Set your sight on a promotion, or even another career, and work toward that goal. While you are on your improvement path, building your skills, you'll become so valuable you can work elsewhere for more pay. Your goal is to become so valuable; competitor companies regularly call to recruit you–just like that golf shop employee. Imagine that feeling. Knowing you could change jobs is powerful and will drastically improve your confidence.

Not having enough time is no excuse. Improve yourself outside of work. Listen to audiobooks or podcasts while traveling. There is an abundance of free knowledge available. There are always ways to get better.

You can find time, no matter what your situation is.

It is surprising how a short, consistent daily time slot can lead to significant accomplishments. Early in my career, I achieved my proudest accomplishment in a daily fifteen-minute habit. Over a six-month period, I developed a comprehensive system for tracking orders and sending out quotations using database software I had never used. My fifteen minutes started at 9:30 am every morning and finished on time at 9:45 am.

I read a thick, mind-numbing programming book on dBASEIII Plus, cover to cover, and completed every exercise. And became the office expert.

Fifteen minutes for 180 days is 45 hours. That's a full, nonstop, no breaks, dedicated week to working on one specific project. Imagine focusing on one project for an entire week without distraction. You could accomplish great things too. So, what's stopping you?

The beauty of the daily fifteen-minute meeting is you can pick up exactly where you stopped yesterday–which is not intuitive. We would think it would take five minutes to get organized, then five minutes to remember what you did yesterday, leaving a scant five minutes to do actual work. In reality, it works as if you are reading a book before bed. If you read it every day, you don't forget. You remember the story and the characters clearly as soon as you pick the book up.

Fifteen-minute projects work the same way. Continue with the same project. If you set aside the same fifteen-minute period every day, I guarantee you will notice dramatic results within two weeks.

YOU WILL GET NOTICED when you take initiative.

I paid attention to my employees actively developing their skills–especially those working on their own time. They were ambitious. I reached out regularly, curious to know what they were learning. Some were learning technical information, others focused on management, while others worked on achieving a new designation that would add to their credentials. They were quietly making themselves better—building their reputation.

. . .

PAUL CORP.

As you build your credentials, consider establishing **your personal corporation. I call mine Paul Corp.**

I found it empowering to consider my career as working for my own corporation. Paul Corp is my definition of how well I'm running all branches of my life: career, finance, health, fitness, social, family and spiritual life.

As part of Your Corp, you get to decide. You decide on your career, how much money you will spend, your fitness level, time watching TV, social media etc. If you decide to stay in a job, that is your decision. If you decide to play video games, watch television or engage in social media more than you know you should, that is also your decision.

In chapter 11: Establishing your Baseline, we look at all aspects of our lives proactively. It's very common for us to develop blind spots, especially in our early adulthood. But before it becomes a lifelong ingrained pattern, it's important to develop balance in your life. Don't ignore a branch too long. That branch will come back later to sting you.

IN MY LAST year working for The DSK Company in Vancouver, I was talking to my sales manager. I forget what the conversation was about, but he mentioned something to the effect that... because I worked for DSK..., and without even thinking about it, I politely corrected him, "I choose to work at DSK. I actually work for myself." I wasn't being arrogant or trying to be difficult. It just popped out of my mouth. I said it in a way where I didn't intend to interrupt the conversation, but it did.

My manager stopped for a second. I watched his expression change. It was as if he was realizing, "OK, so I guess I can't jerk this guy around. He's clearly independent, and clearly ambitious. I need to keep my eye on him."

I had burned into my brain that I was in charge of my career.

I just happened to work in their office.

ONCE YOU ARE on the road to taking responsibility in your career, it is very helpful to understand why you blame and how to recognize it. You might not think you blame, but you do. We all do.

I considered myself extremely positive. My career and personal life were in great shape.

But then I figured out the inner layer of responsibility, and where I wasn't taking control. There was blame, albeit subtle. Once I acknowledged those areas, my ability to take responsibility sent my career to a new level.

* * *

TAKEAWAYS:

- You are in charge of your own personal development and training in your career.
- It's normal to be unclear about your career future.
- Are you coasting in your career? Where can you grow?
- Use daily fifteen-minute increments for skill-building.
- Communicate with your company regarding your career.
- You work for you. You are in charge of your own Paul Corp.

FIGHT FLIGHT FREEZE. BLAME

"*The physical symptoms of fight or flight are what the human body has learned over thousands of years to operate efficiently and at the highest level... anxiety is a cognitive interpretation of that physical response.*" John Eliot, Ph.D., author of *Overachievement: The Science of Working Less to Accomplish More.*

I HANDLED many sticky personnel issues in my company. Usually because no one else wanted to handle them.

I learned about Behavior characteristics, using DISC (see Chapter 9) and had taken a course to be an EQ (Emotional Quotient) Certified Professional Analyst. In my EQ training, we learned about fight-flight-freeze and its connection to negative emotions. EQ also focuses on developing Emotional Intelligence.

WHEN WE EXPERIENCE A NEGATIVE EMOTION, it triggers a physical phenomenon known as a fight-or-flight-or-freeze response.

It's an evolutionary response our ancient ancestors had when imminent physical dangers entered their environment. We and many animals freeze. We remain motionless, hoping to blend into the background when a threat appears, heightening our sight and hearing. Your fight and flight response increases your heart rate and blood flow to the muscles by diverting blood flow from other parts of the body. You are ready to run or fight. Digestion slows down or stops. Adrenaline increases, preparing the body for violent action.

The reaction begins in the amygdala. We consider the amygdala the primitive or reptilian part of the brain as we developed it in the dinosaur years, long ahead of the frontal cerebral cortex. By bypassing your thinking frontal cortex and relying on the amygdala, your brain can send messages a millisecond quicker to your limbs, allowing you to jump out of the way of the oncoming threat.

THINK of your experiences that made you fight-flight or freeze. Especially those that happen instantaneously. Maybe you are afraid of heights or the water? Or are apprehensive about crowds? Maybe it's a person, politician, musician or sports figure you are passionate about? Does some aspect of your financial world scare you? Maybe it's gym class?

WHEN THERE IS **no physical threat:**

Dr. Daniel Goleman referred to experiencing a fight-flight-freeze event when there is no physical threat, as "Amygdala Hijacking" in his book, *Emotional Intelligence: Why It Can Matter More Than IQ*.

In a heated argument, it is difficult to solve complex issues or achieve a win-win solution. Once your amygdala is hijacked, you may not recover for several hours, depending on how significant the emotional event.

In most instances, you can consciously avoid getting hijacked. Just by realizing it is happening, you can lessen the effect of it.

First step: Decide how upset you're going to get.

When someone is frustrating you, you have a decision to make. Will you get upset, and if you do, how upset will you choose to get? Will you be miffed? Irritated? Frustrated? Angry? Seething mad? There is a whole range of emotions you can choose from. Which do you pick?

When you read that question, are you confused? What do you mean, <u>decide</u> how upset I'll get? I just get upset, I don't decide how upset I will get!

Yes, you do. You decide.

You can decide to get more or less frustrated. You can dial down that upsetness and make the difference between a disagreement and a social disaster. We all know we can do this. But can we master it?

When I am hijacked, I make poor decisions. And it happens so easily, and in the silliest circumstances.

Ingrid and I were on vacation driving in Arizona, and we needed to stop for dinner, but I wanted to get to our next destination before sundown. We saw signs for restaurants just off the highway. We took the exit, made a long loop, and followed the signs until we had reached a point that noted the restaurants were another ten-minute drive. No place to turn around. Argh!

I lost it.

Ingrid wanted to discuss which restaurant to go to. I couldn't have a civil conversation. It was clear to me; the town had devised this deception of food being close by, then once it was too late, and impossible to turn around, then they told you how far away the restaurants really were.

Ingrid is familiar with Amygdala Hijacking, and marveled at how upset I was. Even though I knew I was hijacked, I felt agitated for the next hour.

I didn't feel I needed to deal with my upset, because I had acknowledged it. Reality was, I should have done some breathing exercises to calm down a little. (Other quick remedies include light exercise, stretching or going for a short walk.)

FROM THIS MOMENT FORWARD, when you recognize you are experiencing an amygdala hijack, use it as an opportunity to take stock of your physical changes. Can you feel your adrenaline pulsing? Elevated heart rate? Jaw clenched? Senses extra alert? Disregard for anyone talking with you? Are you loud? Autocratic? Or did you retreat? Do you shut down from everyone, with your self-talk sending you into a self-pity spiral? Or do you slam your door and shut the world off?

If you notice a pattern, you can use it as a reminder to stop before you get fully hijacked. If you know your first reaction is to clench your teeth, catalog that critical info.

Another good reason for recognizing amygdala hijacks is to prevent heart attacks and strokes. The Sydney Nursing School at the University of Sydney, Australia, found that episodes of intense anger can act as a trigger for a heart attack. A separate study by researchers from the Harvard School of Public Health in Boston, MA, (March 2014) suggested anger outbursts could raise the risk of heart attack and stroke. *Honor Whiteman, Angry outbursts may raise the risk of heart attack, MedicalNewsToday, February 24, 2015, https://www.medicalnewstoday.com/articles/289864*

One day I watched my boss leave the office so red-faced

angry that he narrowly missed causing an accident backing into the parking lot. When his face got red, we stayed out of his way. In the back of our minds, we all wondered whether one of his outbursts might cause a heart attack. It didn't. He learned how to manage his temper over the years, even without understanding amygdala hijack, but it sure looked to me like he had some close calls.

How do you dial down your anxiety and your blame?

When we go into fight or flight, we will usually blame. When we blame, we can feel our ourselves placing the problem on someone else's shoulders. It feels good, a sense of relief. This is not your problem, it's someone else's. That person is just a jerk. This situation is someone else's fault.

That good feeling doesn't last very long. You might be correct, but you get to be miserably correct. Blame is short-term satisfaction, with back-firing consequences.

My co-worker enjoyed getting under my skin. He would poke me with little jabs about arriving to work later than him and could tell it bothered me. I was clearly outworking him and told him so. He would laugh about me finally rolling out of bed, and I'd retort that I was still at work five hours after he left. It didn't matter. He could see he was getting a rise out of me, and he loved it. Other than that, he was actually a nice guy. I enjoyed him on most other accounts. It was just this one thing. It seems so trivial, but sometimes little things can drive you crazy and ruin friendships. He was having fun. I was not.

I had just begun reading about taking responsibility and the connection between anger and blame. I decided this was a good opportunity to think rationally about this situation. I acknowledged I was agitated. He was getting under my skin, and I would get upset. I was blaming him for being a jerk. I know now; he caused me to experience a mild amygdala hijack. He could make me angry on command. I was the puppet, and he held the strings. He was in control. I was not. So ... that made me his victim.

That made me even angrier. These thoughts were whipping me into a frenzy. Labeling myself as a victim was the tipping point. I did not like that label. I needed to solve this.

I CAME up with an important distinction. <u>I had a better chance to reduce my blame than my anger</u>. Blaming was more of a conscious act. Anger was more emotional. I could be more rational and concentrate on blame. That seemed possible. Trying to control my anger would depend more on my mood. OK, how could I reduce or eliminate blame? And while I was at it, could I use that strategy to deal with other blame issues I had? I was blaming my boss, blaming some friends, blaming my roommates, and blaming all the poor drivers in traffic every day.

As WE BLAME, we give control to the same person who upset us. This is absolutely maddening. And people that enjoy making you crazy know it. They love pushing your buttons, because you react so predictably. It is fun for them. Even more maddening!

The more we blame, the less we are in control of our lives. In fact, we cannot blame without feeling bad ourselves. Try it. Pick someone who upset you. Blame them for the entire problem. It is all their fault. Don't hold back. Let it all go. Put one hundred percent blame on someone. Put your emotion into it. When you're finished, take stock of how you feel for the next five minutes. Do you feel good? Relaxed? No stress?

MY FIRST TEST.
That co-worker was my first test. Here was my thinking process:

1. I knew he wouldn't stop saying stuff to bug me. He was doing it for fun. It wasn't malicious.
2. Why was I upset? I've learned that if you're upset with an insult, it often has some truth in it.
3. I was proud of my work ethic. For him to criticize me made me angry.
4. My boss knew how hard I was working, and his opinion mattered. I didn't need to satisfy my co-worker.
5. If I wanted it to go away, I needed to realize he said it in jest, and not let it bother me.

EVERY PERSON WILL MAKE their own list, with different levels of detail. These were the mental gymnastics I needed to perform. If the comments did not honestly bother me, the insults would stop. I convinced myself I was working hard enough, and enough people knew. Whenever he quipped about me finally getting out of bed, I just agreed with him. I smiled and moved on. It was crucial to truly not be upset with him. I laughed along with him. He tried a few more times in the next two weeks, with similar results. The comments stopped. For good.

Taking responsibility led to taking control of the situation.

. . .

You might say you rarely blame someone, so this won't work for you. Trouble is, we all get frustrated, and we all blame. And we all complain from time to time, but we wouldn't consider ourselves complainers.

Remember, Bulletproofing your Mindset is about you, not them.

If you need to complain or provide criticism, deliver it with good intent. If you are bothered after you criticize someone, you are likely blaming.

If you look for a scapegoat, you are heading toward blame. If you can pinpoint that blame to a person, it's easy for your anger to intensify. When that blame becomes the spoken or written word, you are in full on blame-mode.

In an example of COVID-19, if a political leader does not have the backing of most of the public, they have become a lightning rod for anger and blame. They are an easy target, with so many people looking to hang their blame hat on someone. Most politicians took a beating in the first two years of COVID-19.

In examples where the leader has acted with common sense and integrity, it became less common for them to receive backlash. In British Columbia, our head medical doctor, Dr. Bonnie Henry, is well-liked and has earned the respect of the vast majority of people.

Her message has been consistent. She acts with integrity and empathy. Many of us feel her pain through the tough times and join her in the few small victories she celebrates. She walks her talk and displays real empathy when she talks about those worst affected.

Is it so bad to blame? Isn't it a good form of release, rather than bottling it all in? Won't that cause stress?

Yes, it will cause stress. Yes, you need to deal with it. No, you don't need to blame; you need to take control. Blaming gives control to someone else. Keep driving that home. Once you've blamed, you have allowed someone to control your emotions. You are allowing someone to pull your strings, which may have happened two days ago. Blame controls you. It's supposed to work the other way! That's why you blame, to make it clear it's someone else's fault.

How to use blame to your advantage

We've set the stage for how things go wrong. Now we'll talk about how to turn the tables and start taking control, one situation at a time. Taking control and taking responsibility starts off as a simple strategy and branches out into a group of sub-skills. The more sub-skills you learn, the greater variety of situations you can handle, and the more you become Bulletproof.

But first, in the next chapter, my big mistake.

Takeaways:

1. You decide how upset you will get.
2. Negative events trigger your primitive fight-or-flight-or-freeze response.

3. Your amygdala gets hijacked when you are upset, and there is no physical threat.
4. Blame does not relieve stress, it provides short-term satisfaction, but actually increases stress.
5. You can control blame easier than controlling anger.
6. Take back control using ABC1.

THE BIG MISTAKE

"*In a world that's changing really quickly, the only strategy that is guaranteed to fail is not taking risks.*"
Mark Zuckerberg

THREE YEARS after I started my business, my company was successful in our bid to supply the HVAC equipment for a luxury thirty story condominium, Strava Tower in Vancouver. (Not its real name.)

After we had agreed to a contract price, the contractor sent us an addendum we had not seen. It had changed the thermostats from on-off to modulating. (Modulating valves open and close in small increments, which in theory save energy). They cost significantly more money. The contractor insisted this was part of our contract.

I contacted my suppliers and conducted an in-depth search online to find a solution for one hundred and ninety-six modulating valves and thermostats. There weren't many choices. I found Mento Controls (not their actual name), who, according to their website, had an office in Vancouver. I communicated with them by email, and eventually we agreed to order their equipment. They would provide stock local parts in the event of any failures. Mento promised to deliver the valves in six weeks and the thermostats three weeks after that.

Four weeks later, Mento responded the valves had shipped. They were on a boat. My stomach sank. A boat? Shit. From China? Shit. This was 2001. One hundred and ninety-six electronic modulating valves and thermostats from China had a high probability of failure. Mento reassured me their products were of high quality, and they would stock replacements in their local office. It was too late to change anything at this point. We were already behind schedule.

We installed the products, and within a few weeks we noticed some issues. The worst part was they didn't fail right away. They would work a few weeks, then they would gradually fail. Mento reassured us the product just needed a small redesign. They would upgrade a resistor. The new ones arrived three weeks later, were installed, then all failed three weeks after that. They went through a second redesign. Same result. Slow but steady failures. To make matters worse, the owners now occupied many of the high-end suites, complicating access for our repairs.

Everyone involved was very upset. Lawsuits would be next if this didn't get solved now. I was sick to my stomach. I was pretty certain I'd be paying all of this out of my pocket, and the bill was going to be huge.

I bit the bullet, and replaced them all, before it went too far. The new product was twice the price, plus labor to remove and reinstall thermostats and valves.

Mento admitted they made a mistake, but they didn't "have the money" to pay to fix them. No surprise. Instead, they offered me a discounted price for even more of their equipment to make up for the problem. (Fool me once, shame on you. Fool me twice, shame on me.) We took them to court and won our case for $220,000 for defective products and labor costs to repair and replace. They didn't show up, and we won a default judgment. No surprise, and least of all the surprises, we collected no money from them. On the internet, they looked like they were local, but when it came time to pay, they were not.

THE BUSINESS I built was now on the precipice of bankruptcy. Ingrid and I took a second mortgage and borrowed $50,000 from friends and family so I could make payroll. My primary supplier loaned me $100,000. One of my employees, Nancy, approached me and offered to defer her paycheck for a month if it would help. (It would have helped.)

Deferring to pay my employees for even one paycheck was too much of a stigma in my mind, so I didn't take Nancy up on her offer. I needed to keep my creditors to a minimum. It was already humbling enough. To ask my employees to contribute would be my very last resort. It would cause the line between employer and employee to become fuzzy, affecting that relationship forever. It's tough enough to criticize employees when you have to. It's impossible if they have loaned you money.

I had lots of blame to pass around. It was easy to blame Mento for their poor product. Maybe less obvious was how much blame I put on myself. I put my company in this position. I knew the product seemed too good to be true. If I knew it was from an unreliable source, I never would have bought it. The sales representative avoided mentioning where the products were from and promised that replacements would be available in Vancouver–not true. It doesn't matter. I should have known better. I should have visited their office in Vancouver, instead of just looking at it online. I should have asked specifically where they were manufactured. I could have requested a sample. I should have visited a site where the products were installed or talked to someone who had installed them already.

I was desperate for a solution, and I heard what I wanted to hear.

It was my fault. I had to take one hundred percent responsibility.

IF YOU ALLOW **yourself to focus on blame, it will eat you up.**

I KNEW from my training on blame that if I blamed, this situation would destroy me. If I blamed Mento or myself, I would get depressed and angry.

It would be very easy to revenge the wrong from Mento with whatever resources I could find. The HVAC supply industry is small. I could have easily spread their poor reputation across North America, as we all attend the same conferences. We share information, including the quality and people of the organizations that we work with. If someone is having a poor experience, you could easily hear about it over a beer. And we know how fast bad news travels.

BE careful with sharing negative news.

TALKING about your work issues with a loved one who only wants to protect you may not be a good idea, unless you really need the help. Your loved one will feel your pain, but once you've overcome the issue, you need to make sure they know right away. Otherwise, they may harbor resentment much longer with your co-worker that slighted you. You could be long over the issue, and your spouse is throwing daggers at the holiday party.

The problem is you can't regularly share negative news

without it rubbing off on yourself. If I share my bad news, then I'm the victim.

If I share the bad news and take responsibility for it, then I'm reliving my mistakes. Either way, it reinforces bad feelings and damages my mindset. If I tell the story multiple times and get into the details of the story multiple times, it makes me sound like a complainer.

Talking about our issues can help us process them, but we should limit who we share with. It's best to have a career confidant you can talk to.

* * *

I NEEDED a positive mindset to restart my company. It was critical to concentrate on what I could control. I refused to blame Mento.

A month later, my primary supplier offered to forgive their $100,000 loan and buy out my company, which at the time was very tempting. I went home and talked to Ingrid about the offer. "Ingrid, I made one mistake and can't let it end the dream of owning my company. I know I can turn this around, but we are in this together, and we have to decide together." My wonderful wife agreed to continue our dream.

A YEAR LATER, I visited an art store and bought two beautiful pewter figures that I sent to the company executives that helped me through this challenge. I had them engraved as a thanks for sticking with me. Ingrid and I went out for an amazing celebratory dinner.

Five years later, my company was making more money than I ever dreamed possible. I paid out all our debts. I erased Mento Controls from my thoughts. I could have focused on getting even with the supplier that had screwed me. But I didn't. That doesn't mean I didn't have my moments, because I did.

WHEN YOU MAKE a mistake that is not fixable, you need to make a firm decision and solidify that decision in your memory. You can't be wishy-washy about it. I screwed up ordering that equipment. It was my fault, one hundred percent. And I forgive myself. And I learned from it. That's it. If you allow wiggle room, you're still blaming. If I blame Mento even twenty-five percent, then I'm blaming. It makes me feel weak. A victim.

I took my advice three years later. I ordered an AC unit from a new supplier in Virginia and had a nearby business associate visit the plant to inspect the unit prior to being shipped. It cost me $500 to inspect a $7000 unit, but it was worth the peace of mind. The confidence in the manufacturer led us to buy another $50,000 worth of product from them.

WHEN YOU ARE CLEARLY **the victim.**
When someone else is clearly to blame, and you are clearly the victim, this is where you will need your greatest strength. Mento could easily shoulder all the blame in my story. My guess is you find it hard to believe I could not blame Mento. But I knew I had no choice but to forgive them and myself. I had to put it behind me and move on.

It may take some time, but you need to take responsibility however you can. Whether it's by assuming the other person had issues in their childhood, or it's just their background, or possibly suffer from a mental disorder, or you were in the wrong place at the wrong time, or you were inexperienced, and couldn't know any better. Pick one that resonates with you and stick with it. Make a firm decision. It needs to be firm enough you will always remember why you are responsible. Forgive them and yourself. Let go of the anger you have. You will feel better eventually, and you will free up that angry part of your mind.

What if I blamed Mento?

What if I had blamed Mento completely for the problem, and sought to get even? How could that have affected my personal life? I imagine I would have got angry and depressed. I would be bitter for years. How could that not affect my personal life?

If I walked around crying the blues, lamenting my bad luck, and how I'd been screwed, I don't think even my best friends would put up with me for too long.

Business associates might agree Mento had behaved poorly. Then two minutes later, comment on how I could be so stupid.

But none of that happened. Taking this approach changed my life.

* * *

Takeaways:

- You can take responsibility and save your positive mindset, even when someone else is at fault.
- The more often you tell your sad story, the more it brings you down.
- If you regularly share stories of blame, your friends will become less sympathetic.
- Resolve not to do anyone harm, verbally or otherwise.

NOW IT'S YOUR TURN. TAKE BACK CONTROL

"*Y*ou *will continue to suffer if you have an emotional reaction to everything that is said to you. True power is sitting back and observing things with logic. True power is restraint. If words control you, that means everyone else can control you. Breathe and allow things to pass.*" Warren Buffett.

TAKE a deep breath and acknowledge you are upset. As you feel your blame growing, actively try to reduce that blame. How can you take control of this crazy, emotional situation?

Before your amygdala gets hijacked, let's run through a low stress example using ABC1.

YOU ARE READING A BOOK, doing research in a library. Two people are talking–trying not to be too loud. They are fifty feet away–far enough you can't quietly get their attention. It's now been going on for three minutes and it doesn't look like it's going to wrap up. You try to power your way through the distraction, but it's not working. You are moving quickly toward being upset.

The difference is you now understand ABC1. You can feel your tension (or anger) growing. You know that anger and blame come together. Pinpointing the blame is easy for this situation. It's clearly those two inconsiderate people. C means I need to take Control, and my first method is to use Intent (1). Remember, it's positive intent you are trying to identify.

What positive intent could they have? What comes to mind when you think they are polite people? Maybe you look closer and realize it's a friend of yours? Does that change your opinion? Why would your friend be talking in a library, bothering others around them? Before you read further, come to your own conclusions.

MAYBE THEY DON'T REALIZE they are disturbing anyone. Maybe when they first sat down, there was no one around, so they felt it was OK to talk. Maybe they had intended to just have a brief chat, but it became more involved. Maybe they met serendipitously and haven't seen each other in a long time. Maybe they were waiting for a third person to arrive and are biding their time.

Did you come up with something similar? Once you gave them the benefit of the doubt, did your agitated state dissipate?

IN SOME SITUATIONS, it's best to control your mindset without interacting with others. For example, when you're driving in a car, and you're getting upset in traffic, it is best to calm yourself down. If you can control your road rage, you can control your words. Make a conscious decision you won't let the other driver make you upset. This is an excellent place to practice controlling your mindset.

. . .

WE ALL HAVE moments when we are not on our game. It could be some mild depression, or something has made you unsettled. This is being emotionally hijacked. When we are hijacked, we do not react properly compared to using our thinking brain.

When this happens, train yourself to keep your cool. Channel that extra energy to solve the problem. Your increased self-awareness is key to recognizing situations that may not go well. Take responsibility and take control.

IT WAS me in the library. I tried to get their attention, but finally said, "excuse me!" nicely. It actually took me twice, and I had to say it loud. They were speaking another language and finally heard me. They stopped talking. I smiled with positive intent, not wanting to appear outwardly angry. Just - "Hey. You're talking in a library, and it's not OK. So please stop." They did. (It's amazing how a look with raised eyebrows can convey a specific meaning, as well as cross languages!)

They weren't upset or offended. They looked around and could tell I had the quiet support of other patrons. They got up and left to go–likely to a coffee shop. My fellow library people around me smiled their appreciation to me. That felt good.

I could have said, in a sarcastic tone, "This isn't a coffee shop, but there is one across the street. Why don't you go there?" It will solve the problem, and potentially create a bigger one, depending on how they react. If I made them feel foolish, they may have lashed out with a comment or gesture. Then I would be upset. But none of that happened.

Instead, I achieved four wins. Win for me - the library was now quiet. Win for them - they saved face. Win for the other people in the library, they regained their quiet environment. And last, win for me again because I didn't get upset at all, and I went about my time in the library feeling positive and productive!

If you feel the need to shame people when they clearly are breaking a rule, resist that temptation. In this example, it is crucial to accept that it doesn't matter why they were talking. It does not matter. In most cases, you don't want to know. Assume the best, move on and keep yourself positive.

You might say - "I would never say anything to anyone at the library. The most I would do is to let the librarian know about the problem and have them deal with it." OK, let's say you decide to let the librarian handle it, and they handle it poorly or they take twenty minutes to deal with it. Now the librarian has aggravated you! Maybe they point to you and say, "he's the one that wants you to shut up!" Maybe they are regulars there and are friends with the librarian.

You've given control of a situation to someone else that you could have handled easily and efficiently.

Face-to-face conflict

If you want to scale down your "default upset mode", remember Warren Buffett's advice. Don't let words control you. When someone figuratively slaps you in the face, your instinct is to lash out before they slap you again. If you are face-to-face with someone, and you feel offended or upset, remember you can choose how upset you get.

When you are offended, you are angry and blaming in some form. This happens quickly, so prepare a couple of reactions you can use that won't escalate the situation. You can figure out what type of "angry" you are experiencing later, but for now, when you feel your blood-pressure rising, assume you are in the middle of ABC1.

. . .

A GREAT PLACE TO begin is to take two long seconds while you pay attention to your body language. Assume you misunderstood the person. Don't lean back, cross your arms, and furrow your brow. Instead, lean in, relax your face (which is in an angry contortion), and take a deep breath. That will take two long seconds.

Then, ask a question and listen intently without judgment. You will be agitated, but you're in control for now. (Whoever asks the questions is in control.) By asking for clarification, you are giving both them and you a chance at a new understanding. They may have misspoke, and you have now offered them a chance to soften their message. Keep your mind open and convince yourself you have misunderstood. You could say, "Sorry, I missed what you said. Could you repeat it?" Or "I'm not sure I understand what you're saying, could you say that another way?"

Once they clarify their message, if you remain agitated, you could ask them to elaborate. You could say, "it sounds like we think differently on this subject. I learn from people that think differently from me, so I'm interested to know more." You will probably say it between gritted teeth, but this will give you more time to think.

You could support where you might agree with them, then ask them to elaborate on the subject you disagree with, so they don't get overly defensive. This is difficult, but once you've done it once, you can become addicted to how skilled you become at handling miscommunication. It's very satisfying to take a poor conversation and turn it into a great one. It's a key skill to Bulletproof your Mindset.

* * *

IMAGINE you got off a plane to discover you will miss your connection. Many of the airport's air traffic controllers (ATC's) have called in sick as a negotiation tactic with the union. They are causing flight delays and cancelations throughout the airport. You line up with other unruly passengers to sort out your flight changes. Thirty frustrating minutes later, you get called to the flight desk attendant working on changing flights.

It is clear from the lineup and her obvious stressed condition that she has been doing this non-stop for the last two or three hours. She informs you will miss your overseas flight–the one you booked eleven months ago using all your reward points. Your well-crafted vacation relies on you making that flight. You are about to lose your cool...

YOU CAN IMPROVE the control you have in any situation.

BACK UP THIRTY MINUTES–WHEN you first got in line. While in line, you are watching this situation unfold, and you feel yourself getting upset. That is your trigger to take control. You look up and down the lineup and see others around you feeling the same way. Almost everyone has that look of anger or desperation on their faces. You glance at the flight attendants helping people rearrange flights, and you can see they are frazzled. The longer people wait, the more upset they will be when they meet the attendants. These interactions will not go well.

With your newly developed skills, and sensing your upset state, you decide you are going to take whatever control you can. The ATC's have created a problem you nor the flight attendants can change. So what to do? You have options. Your first choice is to stay cool. Always start with yourself. How are you doing? Are you upset? If you can calm yourself even slightly, you will be more resourceful. Take a few deep breaths.

Acknowledge that strike actions happen, and it's got nothing to do with the attendant you're talking to. Your motivation is to secure your best overseas flight. Recognize that the flight attendant has been talking to upset people for the last two hours straight, and their amygdala is hijacked. You deduce which attendant is in charge–the others are asking them questions. Which attendants are more flustered than others? Which are handling the pressure? When it comes time for you to talk to your attendant, do your homework while in line. How flustered are they and what seniority do they have? You don't know which attendant will serve you, so you're watching them all. (This can take between thirty seconds and three minutes.

The first critical step is to keep calm–the other steps follow. When your turn comes, you are friendly, say hello, ask how they are doing, and make them feel at ease. Smile sincerely and friendly. You spend thirty seconds showing concern and appreciation for their situation. You can tell your story about how long ago you booked the flight, and family waiting for you on the other end. Keep this part short and make sure some of your honest emotion comes through. Don't dwell here too much though, because they've already heard a lot of sob stories. The difference is, you are being polite amid the chaos, and they will appreciate it.

Depending on how critical your situation is, you could help while you were in line. Your smart phone can provide flight options that connect your other flights. If you can provide a flight connection that works and save the attendant looking it up, they might be happy to check that option out–rather than offer the one that arrives ten hours late.

THAT WAS how I handled that situation. I don't think it was heroic, and I didn't do it necessarily to save the attendant some grief. I did it for selfish reasons. It did reduce tension for the attendant. I found an alternative flight while in line; I was pleasant, but to the point with the attendant and presented myself as a reasonable person who was looking for a solution. I got the flight I wanted and saved my other connections. I kept my good attitude, and I helped contribute to the attendant having a break from other angry people. Win-win.

WHAT ABOUT SITUATIONS that are clearly poor intent?

Positive intent works in ninety percent of situations, based on my experience. But what if you are certain someone does not have good intent? What if there is no chance you are mistaken, and this person is mean or inconsiderate? How do you deal with this situation? How do you not get upset with someone like this?

Imagine an ex-colleague is telling unflattering stories about you, and it's clearly with poor intent.

Start with knowing you can control any situation. Next, who are you blaming? That's clearly the ex-colleague. How do I control a situation that has already happened? They said this about me two days ago...

First decide if you are going to let this person continue to control your emotions. And the right answer is, no. However, in order to get your mindset to accept this, you need to make a firm decision.

I'VE HAD this happen to me, and here was my thought process.

This ex-colleague has questionable integrity in my eyes already. They are a competitor. They will embellish a story if they think it will help them. It says more about them than it says about me. I feel sorry for them, that they have to resort to this type of tactic for the sake of trying to secure some business. They must be desperate.

Depending on who gave me the message, I might wonder

why this person is even telling me? Is the messenger enjoying my agitation? Did they defend me? Who else are they telling?

If someone enjoys seeing you uncomfortable, you could decide to ignore them. Does it really matter what someone else thinks of you?

THIS METHOD MAY NOT BE perfect. Come up with your own rationale. I might just say I feel sorry for them, and they must be desperate. That might be enough.

As mentioned in the previous chapter, crystallize your decision so you are no longer reliving your poor relationship each time it comes up. The quicker you can dispose of your upset, the better.

HERE IS A BUSINESS EXAMPLE: Let's say your client says your price is too high, and that's why they are giving the order to your competitor. You do a little digging and find out that wasn't the case. You had the best price. Do you call them back and give them hell?

There are many reasons a client might say this. They may not like you, your company, your products, or they might be the best friend of your competitor. They may not even know you exist and wouldn't recognize you if they met you. Maybe they are a really pleasant person!

The phony excuse grants them an easy way out. They didn't want to explain why your low price wasn't good enough to secure the order. That is a difficult conversation. If they don't like you, assume they don't know the real you. They get their information from your competitor, so no wonder they don't like you. If they are the best friend of your competitor, you may decide to cut your losses and move on.

. . .

THE BEST CUSTOMERS **are the best customers. They just might not be your customers.**

Those customers loyal to your competitors are ultimately who you want for your customers. We all want loyalty. We just don't like it when someone is loyal to our competitor.

It will take a while. It won't happen overnight. But when you eventually turn these best customers over to your side, they will fight as hard as they fought against you previously. The best customers take more time to win over but are worth the effort.

WHAT IF SOMEONE is disparaging you, and they barely know you? Who do they think they are! How dare they!

Wrong.

I know it's our natural reaction, but that was for the old you. Not when you're bulletproof.

Why are you offended by someone you hardly know?

Easier said than done. I get it.

That's why there are degrees to bulletproof your mindset. We need to peel back another layer.

I MADE what I thought was a reasonable comment to someone being discourteous, and they went absolutely ballistic. They ranted and raved at me and my friends for five minutes. We were flabbergasted. We stood there watching this like we were watching a movie. They must have been having a terrible day. It seemed pretty innocent coming out of my mouth, but you never know what is going on in someone else's world.

We all meet people like this. There are jerks everywhere. Sometimes it's us who are the jerks. If you regularly encounter jerks, consider it might be you who is creating the friction. Some people have body language, or use certain phrases that set people off unintentionally. When we do set someone off, it's usually best to not respond at all. Any rebuttal will just lead to a worse situation.

When I encounter an unexpected reaction to something I've said, I have found the best response is to place the blame or responsibility on that person's personal situation, upbringing, or that they've recently experienced an amygdala hijack. I won't be fixing them.

We can't fix everyone. Don't let a rude person ruin your day. If they are this angry and mean, then they are angry and mean, and their lives are likely miserable. There's a saying that goes, "Hurt people hurt people." They want everyone around them to be miserable too. Don't fall into their trap. While it's not a very sympathetic response, I typically save this for people I don't know. I don't share my opinion with them. It's strictly for my mindset.

When a fifteen-year-old teenager that you just encountered says something stupid, you will not be fixing them in this moment. I was that teenager once. I said lots of stupid stuff. Let it go.

When if a co-worker goes off the rails? Can you bring them back to reasonableness? If you are on the receiving end of this, you are going to need all your newfound skills to turn this situation around.

If they accuse you of something egregious, you may want to strike back. That's anger and blame. How do you take control, and how can you even imagine positive intent? The first positive intent you could take is that maybe this person is right. Maybe this person has every reason to think you have done something wrong. Think about their point of view for a minute.

WHAT ABOUT WHEN we are on the giving end of ill intent? We say critical things, and, in that moment, we believe they deserve it. We also believe they should bear the full brunt of our body language, tone, and words. So there is no mistaking they upset us.

So, how do we fix something like this once we've gone too far?

Adjust your body language and your vocal tone. Bring things down a notch. You will probably need to lead with an apology. "Sorry, that was inappropriate." Or "I didn't mean for it to come across that harshly." You could then explain why you were so passionate. "It's a topic I feel strongly about."

You could even apologize for your exuberance, and instead provide a calmer, more conciliatory delivery of your message. One that is not accusing your colleague.

How to take control of your social media

Someone posts on a community group about encountering others in their community, and it didn't go well. Dogs, parking, garbage, lawn care, noise, etc. The post begins with describing the event from their point of view, might include a picture or a news story, and ends with how they believe the other party is guilty. They imply they are right and want you to join them in the condemnation of these less enlightened neighbors. It is rare that someone posts something where they actually want to hear both sides of an argument. Very rare.

Responses come in that pile on the blame and often turn into wanting to shame someone. There could be a few voices asking for tolerance. Depending on how those are worded, the aggressive voices may not be happy with tolerance. Whoever posted the original comment may feel they are entitled to judge the responses.

I have posted tolerance where I can, if I find a community post is negative. I don't feel there are enough calming voices. By allowing a post to remain negative is bad karma for our community.

* * *

WHEN WE GET UPSET, frustrated or angry, we need to use ABC1. Once we know we have experienced A, try to identify who/what we are Blaming. In this case, it's the person who posted, or who they posted about. Since you are sitting at home with your phone, you can decide to take control, and take your time on how to proceed. What positive intent can you imagine? Have you only seen one side of the story? In many of these cases, it's best to pass on commenting. If you don't have the other side of the story in the post, the power of the situation will remain with the person who has posted.

I CHALLENGE you to respond to social media posting in your community with a comment that considers and respects both sides of the story without ridiculing. It is so much easier to throw a dig in with your comment that will set off that person. If you can get a like from both sides of the argument, you have succeeded. As you learn ABC1, tolerance will come naturally to you, as you continue to assume most people have positive intent.

WHEN WE ARE ALONE.

So many of our upset moments happen when we are alone with our thoughts. We think back to a situation and have a conversation with ourselves. We interpret something as negative, and we let it get to us. It might not feel like anger or blame, but if you are upset, you are in ABC1 mode. Interrupt your thinking, realize you are causing yourself to be upset. Take control back.

When you are alone and upset, taking control takes a slightly different twist from ABC1. The critical difference is there is no urgency. When the problem is not talking back to you at the moment, you have time. First, can this wait until tomorrow? If it can, and you can purge it out of your thinking for the moment, that could be the best solution. Make an appointment with yourself to sit at your desk and draw up a plan.

CHECKLIST for when you are alone and have negative thoughts

1. Is this issue urgent? Can I solve it tomorrow so I can sleep? Can I set it aside until I am feeling more resourceful?
2. ABC1: I need to take control. Is it possible there is positive intent?
3. Am I creating a mountain out of a molehill? Is it possible there is no issue at all?
4. How will this eventually get solved? Could I have a positive conversation that would solve the problem? (You are always more likely to be reasonable when speaking directly with someone, rather than an email.)
5. I know that being less emotional and more rational will yield the best outcome. Am I considering which rational strategy I am planning on taking to resolve the issue?

6. Resolve to solve it in the next few days. Issues that fester can gain a life of their own that is ten times worse than the original issue.

AS WE DRIVE OURSELVES SILLY, by imagining highly unlikely, terrible scenarios unfolding in our lives, we really need to laugh at ourselves. We are acting ridiculous, aren't we? We are blowing this way out of proportion. This could be a great episode in a TV comedy.

What happens on comedy TV? Well, they only have a half hour to have a crazy situation occur, laugh about it, then have it resolve. Someone misinterprets a situation. They hear or see something out of context, then get upset. Then they take their misinterpreted viewpoint and compound it. It baffles both sides, until they all finally figure out the situation (the ah-ha moment), everyone apologizes, and there are hugs all around. Usually the person is whole again, and the next episode picks up fresh, without having to resolve the previous episode.

THE ISSUES in our lives aren't so well packaged and are not comedy. Miscommunication lasts much longer. People get offended, brood about it, make judgments about others, often unbeknown to the person who is the source of their anger. Unlike TV, there are consequences for miscommunication. Don't dramatize issues that don't require drama. Solve the issue. Don't wait until next week at the same time, and same channel. Solve it right away.

The more time passes before you solve an issue, the more time you or the other person has to solidify their position. They may have felt slightly offended, but over time, if this feeling is unchallenged, the offence can grow. The details can grow cloudy, and what started out as an innocent misunderstanding turns into a major problem. Don't allow this to happen to you.

Who do you consider to be a communication expert?

I used to consider a professional mediator, the expert communicator. But we need to include a comedian in there, along with a musician or theater performer. Others are TV anchors, human resources specialists, lawyers, teachers and salespeople.

What a mishmash of careers. So who's the best? Is there any clear winner?

There are stars, and duds in every category, aren't there?

What about just regular people, who have their ducks in a row? Those confident, empathetic people that seem to have the world by the tail. Like those small business owners who seem to be living the dream.

We think other people are better communicators than we are. They aren't. In fact, if you adopt these ideas, you will become the person others turn to when things go wrong. Someone who can keep their cool in tough situations.

In the upcoming chapter on personality styles and DISC, you will better understand whether someone's communication style is upsetting you. Are they loud and never listen to you? Or quiet and never express their genuine feelings? Or demanding, and just steamroll over you? Understanding personality styles can help you recognize behavior characteristics, and how some people appear upset when they are not, and vice versa.

* * *

TAKEAWAYS:

1. True power is restraint. Don't let words control you.

2. You decide how upset you will get.
3. Take small steps to control your social media.
4. Give others a chance to change their poor communication.
5. Give yourself a chance to change your own overly exuberant comments.
6. Don't allow issues to spin in your brain too long without dealing with them.
7. Don't allow issues to fester, or they can solidify in other people's minds.
8. The best solution can be to walk away from strangers with ill intent. They likely have their own very heavy burdens to bear.

MCNAUGHTON PLACE

I felt I had done everything right leading up to the tender close for the McNaughton Place project. It was a large air conditioning project in Halifax, and our chances of securing the order were excellent. Our brand was the basis of design, our equipment fit the space perfectly, and our prices were very competitive.

I reviewed the project with several of the bidding contractors, ensuring I had left nothing out. These were all large mechanical contracting companies who had been in business at least ten years. They would bid two or more projects per week and had good instincts for how a project would go and who it best suited. They all assured me it looked like my job, as long as my competitor did nothing stupid.

I felt myself relax, reflecting on those words, "it looks like it's your job, Paul." My preparation was going to pay off. I envisioned the congratulations that would come my way. It would be a great project.

I felt a pang in my gut.

. . .

I WANTED to ignore it and enjoy this moment. My responsibility skill was raising its ugly head. "It's not over until it's over." Where can this go wrong? Don't allow yourself to blame anyone if something unpredictable happens. Didn't you hear that ominous warning from the contractor? "As long as your competitor does nothing stupid..."

Is there anything else you can do to turn this from ninety-five percent success rate to one hundred percent? I didn't want to get angry and blaming after the fact (ABC1). I knew my best chance to affect the outcome was to Control what I could now.

My competitor had bid projects previously when they couldn't meet the specifications–so I had to be prepared for that possibility. In this case, I was certain they had no clue how to price the project. Unless...

HAVE you ever been so sure about something or someone, and then been so wrong? Or have you deleted this from your memory? It's a painful experience to misjudge an important situation. Should you have considered other possibilities? When you are one hundred percent certain about something, are you really? Or does considering the alternate possibility make you feel so uneasy, ignoring it is your only option?

MY NERVOUSNESS STEMMED from the lack of business we had with Stanton Contracting over the last few years. I had a feeling they were working closely with my competitor. What if Stanton leaked my price to them on bid day, and they submitted a lower price? I suspected this had happened before. I immediately felt a pit in my stomach. My five percent failure scenario had grown to twenty percent. This could definitely happen.

I rattled possible solutions around in my head, but I knew I needed to talk to my boss. I summoned up my strength and walked into Ian's office, with that pit growing by the minute.

"I don't think we should bid Stanton on this job. Their estimator could leak our price to our competitor, who I am almost certain, doesn't know how to price this project. It's the only way we will lose this job." I'm sure my face wore the stress I was feeling.

Ian looked at me, took a deep breath, and leaned back in his chair with his hands behind his head. He knew how much effort I already had on the project. I could see the wheels were turning. We had shared the same misgivings about Stanton on a previous project.

A nervous smile started growing across his face, and he said, "OK, but we need to do this right." We talked about strategy for an hour. He suggested I call the big boss at Stanton one hour before job closing to let him know he would have to use our competitor's price. Our competitor was informing all the contractors he was bidding on the project, so Ian reasoned Stanton would still get a price from them.

Stanton would not be happy. But we needed to take a stand.

One hour prior to bid, I called the owner of Stanton. I kept my tone professional and matter of fact. I told him we had grown increasingly concerned that his employee was working with our competitor and had led to a significant lack of trust. I apologized our relationship had come to this point, but because of this we would not bid them. This same competitor was bidding the project, so they would get a price from them. The owner was mostly silent on the other line. "Hopefully we can work better together in the future," I added. I hung up the phone and let out a lengthy breath.

MEANWHILE, our competitor frantically called the other contractors. I warned them this call might come. They offered no help. Some gave him hell for the confusion he had created. They shared these stories with me later, with great amusement.

In the end, I was right. Our competitor didn't know how to bid the project, and in the end, didn't submit a bid. Stanton was furious with them, since without their price they couldn't bid the project. McNeil Mechanical Ltd. won the project, and we supplied the equipment to them.

IT WORKED out but it could have turned out very differently. All my preparations could have been for nothing. Maybe they could bid it? Maybe another contractor could have helped them. It easily could have gone the other way.

I challenge you to read between the lines why the ramifications went far beyond this project. What else happened, do you think? Can you sense how far the influence extended into my career and reputation?

FIRST, it changed how influential people thought about me. Stanton obviously had a new opinion of me, not necessarily a good one. The other contractors who bid the job realized I could be tough–not giving a price to the powerful Stanton was gutsy, maybe stupid. It also reinforced I was technically strong, given I knew my competitor wouldn't understand the project, even though they were adamant they knew what they were doing.

Second, it elevated my status in Ian's eyes. It proved I could think beyond the day-to-day bidding of projects. We were not providing a simple commodity. We provided value in what we did, and we proved it. Plus, by confiding in him, and strategically developing a solution together, it strengthened our business bond, extending his trust in me.

But the biggest influence of all was the effect it had on my self-confidence. I had stuck my neck out far beyond my comfort zone.

I had driven deep into my mindset that there is always something more you can do. And it all happened because I didn't want to blame someone for my failure after the fact. I wanted to take full responsibility. I didn't want to complain. I didn't want to make excuses.

A MONTH LATER, as we were preparing another project, the owner of Stanton called me. He said he would handle the estimates on important projects from that day forward. He asked us to take a leap of faith that our relationship could change. He had suspected his estimator was passing information to our competitor and now had his suspicions verified from multiple sources. He recognized they had given us very few orders over the last few years, and while he couldn't guarantee us any new business, we would get our share if our prices were competitive.

I remember being so impressed with his integrity throughout the conversation, I couldn't help but like the guy. I guess that's why he was the owner of his business. Stanton turned into a top ten client over the next five years.

One more domino fell, all related to a decision not to be complacent, not to blame, and to take control.

YEARS LATER, this idea transformed into a sales system incorporating responsibility that took my company on a ride, that turned our sales company into a powerhouse.

My company had been operating for three years, and I had sales engineers working for me, most of whom followed me from the company I left. We were doing pretty well. We were making inroads. We sold some jobs; we missed some others.

I implemented a system where we shared commissions. We

would split it among us based on each salesperson's overall performance. We would evaluate the percentages every quarter, and decide whether someone deserved more, which, of course, meant someone would get less. Our overall sales volume was booming, so even though someone's percentage might go down, their income typically would not.

This system ensured we wouldn't cut our prices to sell a project to our own customers. This happened regularly at our previous employ and was very frustrating. A fellow salesperson would go into their office, close the door, and drop our price just to their customer. If questioned, he'd say, "Everyone else is doing it. I need to help my guy." The profitability of each project would drop accordingly.

My system didn't go over well with the sales engineers accustomed to "eating what they killed". The stronger the salesperson's ego, the more they wanted the old system.

But the end results were undeniable. Our sales and profitability kept climbing, as was their compensation.

ONE THING WAS MISSING—WE had to rely on our each other's estimate whether they would secure the project with their customer. We would try to read between the lines and offer to help where we could. However, our egos would not let us admit when we were unsure of the outcome. Someone would lose an order and we'd wonder if there was more we could have done.

I decided we needed more accurate feedback. We put up a sales board where we kept track of medium to large projects. Every project that went on our board had a estimated success percentage. Not a unique or earth-shattering idea.

Then I remembered McNaughton Place and taking responsibility. I had assumed the project was ninety-five percent certain, and it nearly got away. We found a way to incorporate this into our sales system.

If someone on my team had a project with ninety-five percent success rate, most people who leave them alone. But we didn't. No matter what the percentage was, we asked how can we improve it? What can go wrong? Have you thought of this possibility? Every week we would go through each project and ask if the percentage has gone up or down, and what caused that change. And how do we improve the current percentage, and is it something we can affect?

Pretty simple, right?

No. Not simple. This is hard.

Pushing your colleagues to first concede they are not completely on top of their job and have to listen to questions week after week was tough. The good news is our intent was good. We wanted each other to secure the project. We had skin in the game. If we could come up with an idea or call on a favor that helped secure the job, we all won.

This became our standard procedure.

We ran that program for three years. Our strategic approach to bidding projects was unparalleled. We covered every angle. We pushed each other. We sold profitable jobs. We made a bunch of money.

As my company grew, I took on a partner, and we slowly abandoned the system. But more on that later.

Takeaways:

- In important situations, take the uncomfortable route, and force yourself to consider the downside of a situation.
- Consider how all parties in a negotiation may affect the outcome.
- Work as a team to maximize your sales strategies

WE ALL NEED A MENTOR

"*A coach is someone who tells you what you don't want to hear, who has you see what you don't want to see, so you can be who you always knew you could be.*" Tom Landry, hall of fame coach, Dallas Cowboys.

MY BUSINESS PARTNER and I were having increasingly intense disputes. We tried resolving them face-to-face, and that didn't go well. We were at an impasse on how we wanted to run the company. Then he didn't want to meet anymore. Finally, in a heated discussion with our head of finance, he told us he wanted me to buy him out.

Buying his shares was in the back of my mind, but once said out loud, I could no longer ignore it. The stakes were at a new level. I needed to clear my head and get some advice.

NO ONE WILL UNDERSTAND the intricacies of your serious business issue as well as you do. There are so many moving pieces. How could anyone else understand? When you share one part of it, that piece gets too much focus. That was just a portion of the puzzle. How can you explain the bigger pieces, if the small ones cause this much headache?

I was having my own headaches. Three years into owning my business, I had no one to talk to about big issues. None of my friends, nor anyone in my company, could understand the complex decisions it took to run a company.

I ATTENDED my friend Lynn's birthday party and met Kevin Armstrong. Kevin told me about his peer advisory group. It seemed they addressed similar issues in their monthly meetings. I apprehensively agreed to join on a trial.

In a typical meeting, each business owner would present an issue and receive advice from the other seven members–all business owners. I watched tough issues discussed and debated right in front of me. Some advice was brutally direct. They knew each other's business. They knew each other's history. And they wanted the best for each other. I found it exhilarating. I joined right away.

I felt like an impostor for the first few months, having only six employees and not feeling I was adding value. Apparently, everyone feels the same when they join. Soon enough, I was contributing. I quickly grew to love it. We had a phrase, "You don't know what you don't know." After twelve years with the group, I was still learning.

Whether it's a peer advisory group, or one of many excellent business or mentoring coaches, you need someone you can share your biggest challenges. The advice cannot be sugar-coated. It must be candid.

Is it worth it to join a peer advisory group or get personal coaching?

WE HIRE ACCOUNTANTS AND LAWYERS, often by the hour. Investment advisers get paid with fees; salespeople get paid commissions. But when you get down to the business of your Paul Corp, we don't invest enough in ourselves. Our rationale is, "How could a stranger understand me or my business well enough to give me important advice?"

ASSUME HIRING a coach can get us a promotion, or a new career that earns $5 more per hour. Based on forty hours a week, and fifty weeks, that works out to $10,000.00. That's every year. If you spent $2000 on coaching, and you earn $10,000 more, that is a 500% Return on Investment (ROI) every year.

If you own a business, what financial impact could a successful business decision have on your company? Typical responses I get are $25,000 to $250,000. Why not spend a percentage to get advice to ensure those numbers actually happen. Or get advice to discourage a bad decision that costs you $200,000 or your entire business.

MY BUSINESS COACH made me money every month. I was ready with my tough questions, and I wanted value. I took those recommendations to my peer-advisory group. They did not sugar coat their opinions to me, or to others. They pushed themselves to follow tough advice. In fact, those companies in our group who followed the advice of the board were some of the highest achievers in their industry.

AFTER THAT INTENSE meeting with my partner, I spoke to Kevin. He suggested I talk to Michael; whose business was in a similar situation two years earlier. Michael had sold a third of his company to a junior owner (partner) three years earlier, and it wasn't working out. They did not share core values on how to run the company.

Michael knew his partner wouldn't accept a reasonable settlement, so he elected to use the shotgun clause as per their partnership agreement. When Michael presented the plan to his peer-advisory group, they unanimously recommended he raise his price. Michael was adamant his partner could not buy him out, because he could not run the company on his own, nor had the money to do so. He reluctantly increased his price, following the advice of his peer advisory group.

The shotgun clause:

In many partnership shareholder agreements, the buy-sell agreement clause can level the playing field in a tough negotiation between partners. The partner who presents the offer will either be successful or has to accept that same offer from the other partner. This ensures the offeror presents a fair offer and must accept either outcome.

When decision day came, Michael's partner bought him out. It devastated Michael. He was financially fortunate he had increased his price but wasn't prepared emotionally.

As Michael recited his side of the story with me, he got choked up, shaking his head in disbelief. The junior owner now owned the company Michael had started from scratch twenty years earlier.

ARMED with the strong possibility my negotiation could go either way, I reviewed our partnership situation and sat down with a lawyer. Given the poor status of our relationship, I had to use the shotgun clause as well. As I prepared the offer, I knew I had to be satisfied with either paying the amount or receiving the amount per share I was offering. It was important to set my emotions aside and deal with the offer. Ingrid and I sat down to discuss the two possibilities with their associated consequences.

One, my partner accepts my offer, and I own the entire company. I estimated this "supposed" best-case scenario would require three years to regain previous profit levels. I predicted sixty-hour work weeks and injecting an additional $200,000 into the company. The road would be bumpy and stressful. The next three years would not be fun. Keeping key staff would be the first task, as partner break-ups impact staff morale.

Option two was my partner buys me out. In that case, I take six months off and look forward to our upcoming New Zealand vacation. We would have solid financial security, where I could retire early if I wanted.

Option two had other benefits: I had been working in the HVAC Equipment sales field for thirty years. I day-dreamed about trying something different, but selling the company was never a possibility. If I didn't sell the company now, selling it later would be difficult. Plus, our business came with sizable risks–as evidenced by the big mistake episode.

SELLING the company was not my original intention, but after forcing myself to consider all outcomes, it was looking like the best option. This turned my thinking upside down. I did not expect to come to this conclusion. Talking with my mentor, then sitting down with Michael, opened my eyes to a different possibility.

I ran the situation past my peer advisory group. The development did not surprise them, as I had been updating them every month. I thought the chance my partner would buy me out was forty percent, sixty percent, for me to buy him out. They had many questions but were most concerned about whether I would experience the same regret Michael had. Would it not demoralize me to sell "my baby" I had started from the basement of my house sixteen years earlier?

I forced myself to consider that question and concluded that I was not enjoying myself in the company's current state. I felt we had been heading in the wrong direction for the last couple of years. Regardless of the outcome, one of us needed to leave the company.

My lawyer and I drew up the paperwork. After much back and forth on what price to offer, I presented my offer. It required a response in thirty days, and it came down to the last day.

BULLETPROOFING MY MINDSET had taught me I needed to be in control of my emotions, in particular, for intense moments. The radical change in my career, between one decision or the other, and not knowing the outcome until the last minute, was enormously stressful. (I'm actually reliving it right now while I write this!)

I went into work that morning and tried to go through my routine, but my eyes were glued to my email inbox.

Bing! An email from my lawyer.

My partner was buying me out.

A mix of emotions rushed through me. My phone rang. It was my lawyer giving me the same news. Was I OK? Yes, I'm fine. (Not really.) As much as I felt I had made the right decision, it would take some time for this to sink in. This was real. I was on vacation.

IN RETROSPECT, my preparation came through. I have no regrets. I made the right decision. I considered the pros and cons, considered my mindset, and considered my personal life. Best, toughest decision I ever made. But that feeling doesn't happen without getting some critical coaching prior to making that decision.

The chance that my business coach, Kevin, was familiar with Michael's business situation was incredibly fortuitous. Speaking with Michael and learning about his unexpected result was valuable. Then experiencing that same scenario and actually being prepared for it was mind boggling. I still shake my head when I think about it.

None of this happens without working with a well plugged-in business coach like Kevin Armstrong, author of The Miracle Manager.

Your own mentor

We all need a Kevin, but we don't think to hire a coach outside of sports. It takes courage to admit and share our vulnerabilities.

* * *

IN OUR MONTHLY peer advisory meetings, each member shared their monthly report. It included sales, financials, and issues that would arise from the previous month. When a new member joins the group, they share mostly good news. The company is doing well. After all, they want to fit in with this impressive group. They believe the group expects them to be successful, with few issues. That attitude changes quickly.

As the new member listens to successful members sharing one significant challenge after another, month after month, it becomes obvious that all companies have issues. If someone successful has problems, I guess it's OK to have problems. Even more amazing, is the most successful members are the ones that follow the advice, especially if there is a consensus from the group.

You would expect them to be set in their ways. How could a bowling alley owner provide worthwhile advice to a geothermal drilling contractor? How could a trucking company owner give advice to a software developer? Yet it happened every month. Businesses share issues such as: sales, operations, banking, hiring and firing, vacations, taxes, etc. All issues where the rules are similar between businesses.

REGARDLESS, if you have a coach now, develop friendships where you can share issues. Take the time to get to know someone's business and career. If you can find a like-minded person in a similar career situation, go out for lunch and share your thoughts. It's best if you aren't in the same industry.

One great place to find an ambitious friend who you may confide in is Toastmasters. John Wedding, *Mighty Bargain Hunter*, referred to Toastmasters as *"The biggest public speaking training bargain on the planet"*.

There are Toastmasters groups in your area. They meet weekly, and the cost is minimal.

I met excellent people at Toastmasters. You can attend your first meeting for free, to see how a meeting works, and see if it is for you. I guarantee you will be pleasantly surprised.

* * *

My first mentor

As a young, ambitious employee, my first boss, Ian, was living in a world that I never thought I would experience. In my eyes, successful entrepreneurs were wealthy, respected, and admired. That seemed unattainable to me. I was very skeptical I could gain entry to this club. Even as I set it as a goal, the chances remained remote in my mind.

Ian encouraged me. It would be hard work and would require exposing myself to financial risks—risks that are not for everyone.

He encouraged me to learn the less glamorous aspects of business. He provided lessons pointing out potential catastrophic consequences. Such as one bankrupt client can bankrupt many of its customers. If you waited too long to pursue that client, your company may not survive either. He wanted me to understand the hidden financial rewards and, importantly, the penalties if you failed.

He also made it clear the rewards were worth the risk. There is nothing more satisfying than knowing you controlled your own destiny.

IAN WAS VERY INVOLVED in our HVAC industry, both locally and nationally. His volunteer boards consumed at least three weeks per year. He said the hidden benefit is the quality of people you meet. You have time to rub shoulders with ambitious people across the country. Some of those people turn into confidants. Since they don't work in the same territory, you can confide in each other freely, providing invaluable insights.

Joining an association, a committee, or as a director can boost your career. These positions elevate your profile and provide free press. The value these associations provided blew me away. I worked my way up through the ranks of our local industry association and was president for a year.

* * *

TAKEAWAYS

1. We can't have all the answers ourselves. A new point of view can be so valuable.
2. When you consider what good advice is worth, mentors can be affordable.
3. Your current boss could be your mentor.
4. Consider joining Toastmasters or a peer advisory group

DISC AND BEHAVIOR ASSESSMENTS

"*There is no such thing as a pure introvert or extrovert. Such a person would be in the lunatic asylum.*" Carl G. Jung.

So FAR, we've talked about mindset, taking responsibility, taking control, and how important it is to have proper mentorship along the way.

Part of self-mentoring is to understand people better. If we are going to become Bulletproof, we must learn to interact effectively with other people, especially in conflict situations. But can you learn people skills from a book? It seems unrealistic since everyone is so different and have such diverse backgrounds.

One of the best people shortcuts readily available is a personality/behavior assessment. It details the natural strengths and weaknesses of someone's behavior compiled neatly in a report. While the boss might gradually appraise an employee's traits, an assessment can provide this information immediately.

A candidate answers an online questionnaire and generates

automated results. An assessment brings data to a science that seems very subjective and helps us appreciate various personalities. (Many coaching or human resource firms provide assessments.)

Behavior and Personality Styles

Dr. William Moulton Marston published *Emotions of Normal People, Richard R. Smith, 1938,* in which his research on observable behavior styles led to today's Four Quadrant Personality Models.

Communication styles are part of our DNA, our fingerprints, and do not transform unless someone experiences a dramatic event. I have studied many assessments, including Myers Briggs, the Driver-Expressive-Amiable-Analytical styles and Kolbe Index. I will focus on the popular **DISC** model, in which I am a certified Professional Behavioral Analyst.

Imagine you have a large square which you then half vertically, then half horizontally so you have four identical size squares. Starting from top left, going clockwise, you have D, I, S, then C. Depending on the strength of the characteristic, someone can score between one and one hundred for each letter, with fifty being the average.

This chapter is not an exhaustive explanation of behavior assessments and DISC. It summarizes what assessments provide and how they help you relate to people.

In this chapter, you will learn how to

- Review a quick method to determine yours and others' DISC style.
- Identify a DISC style using clues from someone's body language.
- Acknowledge your blind spots.
- Identify DISC styles that naturally fit occupations and roles
- Use DISC in your personal life.
- Take responsibility for your own DISC style and how it affects your behavior and communication.

A PERSON who scores high in their Dominant (**D**) style wants results and efficiency. This style enjoys confrontation, is very direct, impatient, and to the point. They love challenges and are quickest of all styles to anger. Think of Tiger Woods (golfer), Charlie Sheen (actor), or Gordon Ramsay (chef).

A high Influencer (**I**) style craves social interactions, having fun, and is optimistic. They are spontaneous in their decision making and are considered dreamers. Think Will Ferrell (actor), Jay Leno or Ellen DeGeneres (TV hosts.)

These two styles, Dominant and Influencer, are typically extroverts.

Someone who is a high Steadiness (**S**) style is patient, stable, sincere, relaxed and modest. This style does not like confrontation. Their world is their relationships, which they want to operate in harmony. They want a solution that makes the most people happy. They are more hesitant to change than other styles and are best at taking a project to completion. Think of actor Tom Hanks, Mr. Rogers, or Barbara Bush.

Last, the high Compliant (C) style is methodical, courteous, restrained, and often a perfectionist. They make slow, deliberate decisions and pride themselves on accuracy. Think of Bill Gates,

Elon Musk, Johnny Depp or Jim Parsons (as Sheldon Cooper). People that love programming computers and coding will usually have their Compliant score above fifty percent. They follow rules and will drive the most practical or reliable vehicle.

Steadiness and Compliant styles are typically introverts.

WE ALL HAVE a combination of introvert and extrovert tendencies, but for the sake of our discussion I will say "introvert" or "extrovert" when I mean "someone who has an inclination toward introversion or extroversion."

IN SOME SOCIETIES, we confuse introversion with shyness. Introversion doesn't mean you don't like people, you just like them differently from an extrovert. An introvert would go to a party and enjoy themselves immensely if they could find a quiet conversation, preferably one on one, away from the chaos.

In North America, introverts have a bad rap, whereas in many areas of Asia, they treat introverts with honor and respect.

Susan Cain, the author of *Quiet: The Power of Introverts in a World that Can't Stop Talking,* provides the following differentiation: "Introverts prefer lower-stimulation environments, that's where they feel at their most alive. Whereas extroverts crave stimulation in order to feel at their best."

Introverts are those people who wear headphones when asked to work in an open concept setting. The loss of productivity experienced by the introverts overshadows the collaboration you are hoping to achieve, because they are more adversely affected by the noise and distractions. COVID-19 required many people to work from home and has been a blessing for many introverts.

. . .

THE NEXT TIME you have a brain-storming session, don't allow everyone to yell their thoughts out. You will never hear from the introverts! They need an environment that allows them to express themselves at their own pace. Instead, give each person an opportunity to speak up in their turn, or even better, allow everyone some time ahead of the meeting to brainstorm on their own. You will get great ideas from your introverts.

If you are a strong introvert, acting like an extrovert is difficult—or vice versa. Robin Williams was both wildly outgoing and painfully introverted, *Dave Itzkoff, Robin (2018)*. He was a self-confessed introvert who cherished his alone time to recharge and used that time to tap into his creativity. He created his own imaginary world with imaginary characters, who he could converse with for twenty minutes non-stop.

His ability to think on his feet with a live audience, were borderline genius, according to renowned comedians who watched his work. The smallest quip or comment from the crowd would set loose a reaction that was difficult to imagine being spontaneous. Those live shows took their toll and required some serious down time for Robin the next day.

KEEP that in mind when you bring your introvert spouse to a cocktail party where they won't know anyone. By the end of the evening, they can be stressed and exhausted.

Extroverted small business owners will tell you they can hunker down and deal with analytical details when they have to. What they won't tell you is how much it wears them out.

TO REMEMBER which letters in DISC are extroverts and introverts, the first two letters, D and I, are for the extroverts, because they want to be first! S and C are the introverts—the supporting cast—the last two letters of DISC.

HERE IS **a method for determining your behavior style.**

Ask four people you know well if they would answer the following questions for you. They need to respond with a number from one to one hundred without saying fifty.

This example will provide some information but is not a substitute for an assessment conducted by a professional.

1. Do I speak, act, and behave at a quick pace or at a steady, deliberate pace? Score one hundred points for an extremely quick pace, and one for a very slow, deliberate pace. If it's a toss-up, pick forty-five or fifty-five.
2. Am I very interested in other people, like to talk about them, am open and cooperative, and have no problem speaking up? Or am I more interested in getting tasks done, relying on facts and figures–preferring my communication one on one, or fine to keep to myself? Score one hundred for extremely people oriented, one for prefer communication one on one, and more interested in facts.

If you speak and act at a quick pace, you are likely a Dominant or Influencer. If the responses suggest you are slower paced, you would be Steady or Compliant. If they suggest you like to chat more often about people, are open and cooperative, then you are Influencer or Steady. If they were more about facts and tasks, and are more challenging, you are likely Dominant or Compliant. These simple questions could place you in one box, or two boxes.

You can get a more accurate assessment if you perform this exercise for each of your friends. Your friends' lens affects how they perceive your style. If they are very quick paced themselves, they may see you as average paced, when in fact you are quick paced, just not as quick as them. Again, this is not a perfect analysis, but a tool to give you an overview.

You are multiple styles. **Scores are important.**

As you dig deeper into styles, you'll learn you are not one style alone. The DISC assessment provides scores for each letter, D-I-S-C. It's common to have scores above fifty percent in two or more styles. The intensity of that style is important.

For instance, my friend Gary's **D**ominant score is seventy-six percent, and his **I**nfluencer score is ninety-three percent. The combination of High **D** and High **I** shows Gary is a strong extrovert. That is not a secret to anyone; Gary has strong opinions on most things. If you golf with Gary, and you expect him to keep quiet, ... you will have to tell him–maybe twice. He has a heart of gold, is great fun, and a solid friend.

If you didn't understand styles and are an introvert, you might not have the patience to be with a strong extrovert, and you would miss the fun times you could have together.

When we meet people in a social environment, we usually keep an open mind. We are accepting and admiring of someone's characteristics. We might like them because they are just like us, or different from us. As we get to know each other better, we are experiencing the "honeymoon phase" of a personal relationship.

Introverts love having an extroverted friend to keep conversations going when they are stuck for words. They are happy to listen until they are ready to contribute. Getting into the details of subjects that interest them are some of the best conversations for them.

As we spend more time together, and the honeymoon wears off, we become comfortable sharing our true selves and allow our full personality to be shared. As we do, the annoying side of our personalities rears its ugly head. We expect our honeymoon partner to accept this side of us, ... but will they?

You could put the onus on them, but you are the one who now knows more about personality styles than they do. You understand how to take responsibility, take control, and find solutions to communicate how your styles are introducing conflict in your relationship.

Exercise

You already have a relationship which is strained for these very reasons. We all do. Can you think of it now? Even a little strained?

The next time you can feel yourself strained when speaking with a friend, you know what to do. ABC1. Reduce your blame by finding good intent.

Let's say someone is acting overly worried for someone's health, or overly caring and sympathetic. You listen for a short while, but it's going on too long. It's rubbing you the wrong way. This person is probably a high Steadiness. So, instead of ridiculing them for being over-sensitive or worried, thank them for their concern, and try to move the conversation away from this topic.

If you want to provide feedback, you could say that while you realize they are very caring, you may not share those feelings. They may have their opinion, but you can also have yours. And yours may be completely opposite to them. But that doesn't mean you have to argue about it. They can be their way, and you can be yours. Agree to disagree, instead of chastising each other and straining the relationship.

How can you observe other DISC styles?

Everyone can read other people. It is a survival skill. It's not a skill reserved for a professional interrogator. When you mention a person looked kind of shifty, or that they seemed depressed or anxious, you are picking up their signals. Professional interrogators pick up many of the same signals you do. The difference is they have references for those signals and turn them into conscious observations.

RECENT STUDIES HAVE SHOWN that when the human brain is observing objects, it is on medium alert. The brain goes on high alert when we see another human, and in particular a human face. The brain activity takes a noticeable jump. It is a survival instinct assessing whether this person is a friend, threat, or potential mate.

We do this at remarkable speed. If you take a two second glance at someone, you can pick up an extraordinary amount of information. We are looking for clues such as age, physicality, and fluidity of movement. You may also pick up awkward or confident movement, a deformity or an injury. If your eyes meet for any length of time, you experience even deeper perceptions.

Try it for yourself. Take a one second glance at someone, turn away and tabulate your observations. It is uncanny how good we are at this. It should be a party trick!

BODY LANGUAGE

We all give away clues. We don't conceal our mannerisms, especially outside of home, because it is so rare we get caught and called out. For example, if someone gets rattled, they display unmistakable body language. They might cross their arms, stiffen their body, furrow their brow and mouth. We know we upset them.

Some introverts prefer to communicate with their body, rather than their language. Rather than having to voice their displeasure, they are hoping you pick up on their signals! Even in a case where their body language is so strong and obvious, it is rare that someone will call out what they are observing, for instance, "Hey, I can see we upset you!"

If you feel caught, you might scrutinize yourself to see how your emotions are being betrayed. But this is rare. In those cases where our body language betrays us, we will remember to be more subtle next time.

WHEN TWO PEOPLE SIT TOGETHER, are their shoulders level to each other, or is one side up, displaying an aversion for the other. Is someone leaning back, or leaning into a conversation? What about eye contact? Is it engaged, uncomfortable, distracted or bored? If the person is standing, is the stance engaged, or tired?

Make an effort to watch body language, especially when you are in a social gathering. Watch another group from a distance and observe.

DISTINCT BEHAVIOR STYLES **exhibit distinct body language.**

You have seen a Dominant style show strong gestures without even realizing she is doing it. She dresses businesslike and gets right to the point. Are you annoyed by this? Too bad! This is who she is! She will not change. Since you've studied DISC and body language, you have an upper hand. You can be direct and engage in a dispute without offending her. High intensity Dominant styles love confrontation and intense discussions. They live for this. You can push them as long as you don't wrestle control away from them, and your argument is to the point–no long-winded stories! Under stress, the Dominant will get more critical, blunt and uncooperative. If you know a

Dominant, and their face gets red, prepare yourself for a blow-up.

The Influencer dress is stylish and fashionable, and when they walk in the room, they act like they have raised the curtain! I'm here! They use lots of gestures, are gregarious, and want to meet people! OK, same drill–are you annoyed by this? Too bad. She's not changing either! If you can put on your extrovert hat for five minutes, try to be friendly and open. Arms open, back-slaps and hugs are common to this person. When under stress, the Influencer will get sarcastic and demanding. As their trust level lessens further, they are likely to criticize others and be combative. Watch for these clues.

The Steadiness dress is casual and conforming. He will walk in low key, relaxed and friendly. He may come across reserved and shy of crowds but loves relationships. He prefers a one-on-one discussion. He will remember all the social details of people he meets and is not in a hurry. Is your style different from his? Too bad! Steadiness types are exceptional poker players as they tune into theirs' and others' emotions. Don't be preoccupied when chatting with him, or his radar will go up. He will excuse himself out of your insincere conversation. Instead, talk with him about relationships. Under stress, the Steady will be submissive. When you notice them no longer engaged or retreating, it is likely something has upset them. In these situations, you will notice they are more hesitant or apologetic.

The Compliant dress is formal and conservative. Social outings are not his favorite thing to do. He will enter with as little fanfare as possible, allowing whoever he is with to do the talking. He is observing everything, though. At a business gathering, he will greet everyone. He doesn't want surprises and much prefers predictability. He either uses no gestures, or very reserved ones. The Compliant appreciates being introduced, but don't exaggerate who they are–be accurate. When under stress, the Compliant will withdraw or recite details. If someone criticizes them, they can disengage and may leave the room. When pushed to defend themselves, they will quote rules and procedures.

THERE IS much to learn about behavior styles both online and in books. I would encourage you to sign-up for an assessment, to learn more about yourself. You will want to take one that measures intensity (or percent) of style, not just one that gives you letter designating a style.

YOUR OWN STRENGTHS and weaknesses

If you complete an assessment, your focus will be on how you fit into the assessed model. You will question whether the assessment report accurately represents you. This is normal.

When I completed my first behavior assessment shortly after I started my career, I found it fascinating. It helped me understand my behaviors, strengths, and weaknesses as a sales engineer. I agreed with the results, which suggested I was high Influencer and enjoyed meeting new people.

My high Influencer style has its drawbacks. My style means I'm probably talking too much and not listening enough. I can have a hard time focusing on something that is not interesting to me. I need to listen more carefully and be more empathetic. I am more trusting than others, believing that things should go fine, whereas others might feel I am not thinking realistically. I am not detailed-oriented and am more of a rule-breaker than a rule-follower.

My secondary style is Dominant. I have a habit of getting right to the point and forgetting to start an email conversation with a greeting. I know others don't appreciate that. By recognizing who I am, I stop fighting myself and make a point of being more personable, especially in short interactions. I know these traits can be very annoying to others, and I want to be better.

> Individuals knowing and valuing their own personality style is highly beneficial. *Varvel, T., Adams, S. G., Pridie, S. J., & Ulloa, B. C., 2004. Team effectiveness and individual Myers-Briggs personality dimensions. Journal of Management in Engineering, pp. 141-146.*

WE NOTICE other's blind spots. We might give them a jab about being bad with numbers, or lacking empathy, or being loud. But we know we have them too. We might think they are so minor that they're barely worth mentioning.

During an assessment debrief I facilitated, a high Dominant client said his friend accused him of using sarcastic and belittling language. He acknowledged the criticism and agreed he should work on it. Two days later, I was in a meeting with him and his team, and he was repeatedly sarcastic and critical, right in front of me. I was dumbfounded. I gave him my best scowl, but he was oblivious. His employer and I worked together to address the issue with him, and is a classic example of a blindspot.

. . .

THE GOAL IS NOT to fix all the downsides of our behavior style. The goal is to first acknowledge we have blind spots.

If you know you have a tendency to withdraw from a conflict, you could equate "leaving the room when uncomfortable" as your trigger. When that situation arises, you could tell yourself, "Normally I would leave the room in circumstances like these, but I don't believe that will solve the issue. Let's see if we can work things out respectfully."

But they are blind spots for a reason. You may need a trusted friend to point out your undesirable behavior, because you don't even know you're doing it. Sometimes, it will require an intervention from several people.

* * *

DOES your style fit your occupation?

I have met successful people, with all different styles, in all different occupations. I have met extrovert accountants and engineers, and introvert salespeople. That being said, as someone's career progresses, they will best succeed using their natural skills.

There is a large percentage of introvert engineers. Engineering companies value technically inclined employees, but also need a few people who can relate well with clients.

Harold is a partner in an engineering firm and is naturally outgoing and loves meeting and interacting with clients. His partners are also good with clients, but not to the same degree as Harold. Harold will think and speak on his feet, loves to joke around, and is usually the center of attention.

Harold's partners enjoy the technical challenge and are more focused on that side of the business. As a team, they satisfy the technical and relationship-building part of their business, which has resulted in their firm's long-term success.

In an accounting firm, David is the leader, and possesses

strong leadership skill. He has a strong Dominant characteristic which is critically important in a firm where most accountants have strong Compliant characteristics, who typically are not decisive. His ability to push his high Compliant staff to make decisions, are key to the firm's success.

In a sales engineering role, Wayne may have lower extrovert characteristics than some of his colleagues, but his ability to dive into details makes him a favorite of the mechanical engineers. Those engineers feel the typical salesperson doesn't value the details as much as Wayne.

Use the DISC diversity of your team.

In companies with multiple partners, like an accounting or legal firm, there is an expectation for all partners to fulfill all roles, with little regard to their natural style. Since many firms never conduct proper DISC assessments, a partner may not know where their natural strengths lay.

Inevitably, the extrovert partner (high D or high I) has no trouble in securing new clients, but is not as good with retaining those clients, especially those that demand attention to detail. The introvert partner (high S or high C) is slower in establishing clients, gaining less attention than the quick-start extrovert, but once they get going, they take great care of that client, paying attention to detail.

However, if the introvert has an extrovert client, they may not satisfy the client's desire for an open, fun relationship. That could lead to that client considering switching firms, especially when they meet an extrovert competitor at an event, who they hit it off with. This is an over-simplification, but you get the idea.

. . .

IF THE PARTNERS hire their own staff without using an assessment, they have a tendency to hire people like them. They relate well. They share the same strengths. They like each other. But that creates a unique problem. Everyone the same is not good. One partner's team is full of extroverts, the other's introverts. Therefore, it's good to have several people assess a candidate, and while they should not completely base the decision on style, it is wise to consider it.

Once you've identified the unique skills of your partners, you can group clients that have similar communication styles. Place the detailed oriented architect with the detailed oriented mechanical engineer. Have the outgoing property manager connect with your outgoing partner. It just makes sense–everyone benefits.

It seems simple, but it doesn't happen that way in practice. If you haven't taken these assessments, egos get in the way. We all believe we can relate to everyone. We all believe we can be natural salespeople, but it's just not the case.

Instead, improve your chances and use the diversity of your team to connect to a client. At the very least, ensure the subordinates are well-matched to the client's subordinates. If you cannot match them, then provide training to understand styles.

Greg Macdonald

When I started my career at DSK Company in the Halifax sales office, one of our important clients was Greg MacDonald of Western Plumbing. My boss and he did not get along. After a heated conversation between them, my boss threw the file at me and said, "He's all yours!"

I was excited, but Greg didn't appreciate his account being handed down to the junior guy. He acted professionally, but that didn't mean he was pleasant. He had no problems pointing out my failings: my quotations were incomplete, the shop drawings we submitted were inadequate, and our deliveries were always too long. His purchase orders were three pages long, instead of the more common half-page purchase orders, and he filled them with contentious conditions. I had to go through them line by line and argue with him at every point. Plus, I was only getting drips and drabs of his business.

Twelve months earlier, when I started my career with DSK Company, they had me complete a behavior assessment. It wasn't as comprehensive as reports are today, but it gave me an idea of my style. It helped me realize other people had distinct styles and preferred I communicate with them in their style-not my style. I set aside what I'd learned, not actively using it in my sales effort. It didn't seem all that practical.

One day, my frustration with Greg hit a tipping point. "Hi Greg! I hope you are having a great day today! How was your weekend?"

"Fine."

Undaunted, I explained how my weekend went, trying to be as entertaining as I could be.

Exasperated, he finally interrupted me and said, "When is my air conditioning unit going to get here? You said it would ship today."

I stammered something and told him I'd have to get back to him. I hung up and shook my head. "This guy has no personality." I sat there, brainstorming how to get more business from this important client, and a light came on.

He wanted accurate facts, not guesses. He wanted me to be thorough. Greg never talked about people and couldn't care less about my weekend. I thought back to behavior styles, and I almost fell out of my seat. He is high Compliant style!

I reminisced about our interactions to date, and it made complete sense. His purchase orders were perfect and overly detailed; he took forever to decide; he always needed more information from me; and he based any decision on logic–no emotion. He checked all the boxes as a Compliant.

My Influencer style was the same as my boss's (more expressive and personal), so it was no wonder we both agitated him. Opposite behavior styles do not attract when negotiating! OK, so now what? I needed to do more research on styles. I listened to Dr. Tony Alessandra and Jim Cathcart's audiobook *Relationship Strategies* and Jim Cathcart's book *Relationship Selling: How to Get and Keep Customers*. They gave me some excellent ideas about how I should deal with Greg's style. Some of those tips include:

- Take time to be accurate.
- Give him evidence and service to make decisions.
- Make sure he can justify his decision logically.
- Be aware that he fears criticism.
- Emphasize accuracy, quality and reliability,
- present obvious disadvantages.

I felt energized by this revelation and excited to try it out.

A MONTH LATER, Greg wanted a price for a steam heat transfer coil–a small retrofit project. To price and select a coil, I ran the information through our engineering selection program. I was about to send Greg a quotation but recalled my revelation. I decided I would try to appeal to his Compliant style.

I sent him the complete two-page computer heat transfer performance printout. The printout looked very much like an engineer's dream: A lot of numbers and at least thirty acronyms–not designed for a typical mechanical contractor customer.

The output provided three coil choices. I circled the best choice, scribbled the price on the bottom of the printout, and sent it. I was giggling to myself as I watched it go. I'll at least get a reaction from this stodgy guy!

Thirty minutes later, Greg called me. "Tell me what all these abbreviations mean."

Wow. I was stunned.

He is SO Compliant! I walked him through the more important acronyms, what each meant, and how important each value was.

He wanted more. "What if we changed some inputs? What are the other steam coil prices?"

Five minutes later, once Greg had all his answers, he couldn't resist himself. "Is that your best price?" I could hear the smile in his voice.

"Yes," I smiled back.

"Well, you have the order."

"Thanks Greg!"

I made a friend that day.

Our relationship changed from that point on. I never spoke to him without considering his style again. I put my "Greg" hat on. I was thorough; I didn't skip steps; I provided updates when I said I would or didn't ramble about my weekend. This did not come naturally to me. I had to force myself over our next half-dozen conversations.

Greg preferred we work out the details on the purchase order so we could just sign it and return it–pristine and perfect. He didn't like me messing up his document. I stopped being frustrated and grew to like him. He was who he was. Our behavior styles clashed, but he was consistent and predictable. He became one of my best clients.

My boss would hear Greg and I on the phone laughing about something, and he'd shake his head. I think most salespeople that called on him were the Influencer style that clashed with him. I was the one who adapted to his style and understood what was important to him. On that day, I realized how crucial it was to understand my clients' behavior styles.

DISC IN YOUR PERSONAL LIFE.

A few years into identifying clients' styles, I met my wife-to-be, Ingrid. On our second date, I learned many wonderful things about her. I was really doing my best to make a good impression, realizing I had met someone very special.

I was evaluating a client's DISC style earlier in the day, so that was fresh in my brain. I thought about Ingrid's fast-paced, direct to the point mannerisms. This probably meant her primary style was Dominant. She was a good listener who talked about her close friends, which could mean a secondary Steadiness style.

We quickly grew close and were engaged six months later.

I DIDN'T DWELL on these observations, but from time to time, I would notice that she acted consistently with her D and S styles.

Understanding her behavior style was very helpful later on in our relationship, especially when we had a disagreement.

She is not shy to share her side of the story and takes a strong stand on topics she is comfortable discussing. Her Dominant style does not want me to meet her with my competing Dominant behavior. When it happens, it conflicts with her high Steadiness style, that usually prefers harmony in her relationships. She is just making a point and wants to be sure I am hearing her.

I have learned that I am best off allowing her to blow off steam and return to an energetic discussion an hour or two later.

Over time, Ingrid has learned my high Influencer style means I enjoy meeting people, socializing, and going to parties.

When we're out with friends, she is in her element and loves to chat, dance and have fun. When we go to a gathering of unfamiliar people, I'll stay with her for at least the first fifteen minutes while we mingle. Depending on how many people she might know at the party, I know whether she'll want me to check in with her every so often. Once she's settled in with a person or two she knows, I will wander around and introduce myself to other people. When it's time to go, she prefers I initiate leaving the party and is always ready to go before I am!

In social interaction, I prefer more get-togethers than she does. I know I can't spring these on her. If I give her some time to think it over, the likelihood of it happening goes up. We have figured out situations like this over twenty-nine years of marriage, and still work at it.

BEWARE YOUR DIAGONALLY OPPOSITE!

In the box we drew earlier, it showed that D was diagonally opposite to S, and I was opposite to C. If someone has a strong D trait, for example, they may notice they get into regular conflict with someone who has a strong S trait. Same for the I and C. The stronger the trait, the more likely there will be conflict.

The reasoning is simple, if you are a strong D, thus you are fast-paced, and are more about facts. If you are having an interaction with someone who has a slower pace and is more interested in talking about people and feelings, you will both experience frustration.

The same for the strong Influencer being open, liking to talk about people, and uninterested in details, talking with the reserved, high Compliant, who wants to talk facts and figures. Keep in mind, if someone regularly frustrates you, they may be your opposite style.

. . .

THERE IS a tendency to have a spousal relationship with someone whose style is not the same. We often prefer the long-term company of someone whose style is next to our dominant trait. So, a strong Dominant person would enjoy a high Influencer because they are fast paced. Or they might enjoy a high Compliant style, who values facts and details, although they aren't as outgoing. A mix of introverts and extroverts is common, which provides them the amount of talk time both parties enjoy. The high I wants to talk a lot, the high C, not as much. Everyone's happy.

***

TAKEAWAYS:

- A personality behavior assessment is the best shortcut for understanding people.
- Our DISC style is part of our DNA, like our fingerprints
- Understanding extroverts and introverts is important on many levels.
- It pays to understand your own DISC style.
- Use DISC in your personal life
- You can learn to identify other people's DISC styles, using their clothing and style, as well as their body language.
- Different styles can succeed in the same business, but ideally, you have a team with balanced styles to help you get along with the greatest number of clients.
- Beware your diagonally opposite style in DISC. You are likely antagonizing each other.

IMPLEMENTATION OF DISC

"*Knowledge is not power. Knowledge is only potential power. Action is power.*" Tony Robbins, Personal Power.

ONCE YOU'VE MADE the effort of identifying at least one friend and one acquaintance's behavior style, you have opened another advanced layer to Bulletproof your Mindset. When you experience the flashes of insight I predict, you will want to practice this with all the important people in your life.

Resist the temptation to make fun of the other person. It's OK if you know their style, but don't rub it in their faces. Instead, use it to appreciate the other person and their natural talents. Use it to connect with them, as well as to communicate that you don't have those same skills.

People who don't take responsibility will dismiss behavior styles with excuses so they can continue their lazy form of communication. They give up trying to understand why others think differently than they do. They get frustrated, acting like a victim of other people's poor communication skills.

They dismiss assessments by saying, "Oh, I do that already" or "I've read books like that." Or commonly, "I took the Myers-Brigg self-assessment." My reply is, apparently, everyone understands this stuff. Then why doesn't anyone use it?

How do you explain I was Greg's only friend in a city full of salespeople? My boss, a very successful owner of a technical sales business, received training in behavior styles and had taken the same assessment as me. He had called on Greg for ten years. What was his excuse? Why did it take me six months to figure it out? What was my excuse? Knowing is not enough.

I WILL PREPARE you for some thoughts as you consider practicing this skill, because they are normal as well.

EXCUSE 1: People should accept me the way I am, and I should accept them.

We should all get along with all different behavior styles. However, we already discovered that we don't.

I agree we should be more accepting, and the way we do that is with more knowledge of people around us. When someone is rubbing us the wrong way, we can now partially attribute that to a behavior style. That is acceptance.

If you decide others need to accept you the way you are, that is not being Bulletproof either. Being Bulletproof is not about being indestructible or impenetrable. It is the opposite. It is being vulnerable and courageous.

To live a full life, you must cast off your restraints and armor. Take risks to grow and fulfill your potential. We all want to grow. We want to get better. When you encounter someone who you can't figure out—you can't give up. You cannot blame the other person's poor communication.

When you meet someone that seems to take forever to

decide, dig deep and deduce they likely have a low Dominant style. These same people have great strengths. They are slow to get angry and prefer to analyze situations. You can take comfort in knowing they have thought out any decision they have made and could provide their complete analysis if you are interested.

By taking responsibility, you may need to help the low Dominant to decide by walking them through the options and helping them see why deciding now logically makes sense–all the while not pressuring them excessively. If you are coming from a non-judgmental perspective, you won't get upset. You will accept them for who they are. The other person will sense your good intent and be more open and agreeable to the conversation.

EXCUSE 2: **I can't keep straight which styles do what.**
This was the case for me early on. It's difficult to keep these styles straight. In the beginning, I needed reminders. I started by separating the circle into halves.

The top half is D and I are extrovert/assertive (the first two letters), S and C are the bottom half and are introverts/reserved (the supporting, last two letters). The Left half is Task-focused vs. Right half, People-focused.

I could almost always identify one of those four. That would at least help me understand some of this person's tendencies. Just knowing someone was a people person was an excellent clue. I would focus on which person had bought this product, or who we both knew. If I was right, it would energize them to continue the conversation about people.

Review a few DISC images online. Print them out and keep a cheat sheet beside your desk. I needed these initially as I struggled to remember key characteristics of each style.

. . .

Excuse 3: Do I really want to work this hard on my relationships?

I hear you. It's one more thing in a very busy life. I would rather not have to do this. And that's OK. You don't have to. However, when you find you aren't connecting with someone, or you notice someone important to you is agitating you regularly, remember you can go back to this information. Remember also that not appreciating your own style, and your own blind spots, can cause issues you don't even know you are causing.

Regardless, I highly encourage you to try it at least once. The results will inspire you to use it more often.

Excuse 4: Using personality styles is manipulation.

Is using DISC manipulation? You and everyone else around us prefer to work with someone who communicates with them in the manner they like. Just like Greg and me. We became buddies, and that was not manipulation. He wasn't able (or maybe willing) to adapt to my style, so I adapted to his, and we became friends.

We change our behavior for people we care about. When we meet our spouse's parents for the first time, we are on our best behavior. What does that mean? It means we think before we talk. We listen. We notice what is acceptable and what is not. We mind our manners.

Is this manipulation? Maybe. But the reason it works is you are appreciating others, instead of being wrapped up in your own world. It's just good manners, isn't it?

How important is using DISC at work? Can it help someone's career?

A company hired Jacob, a sales engineer. He was a hard

worker and a likable guy. After two years of working, he was having trouble connecting with clients.

He had spent one-third of his time over a three-month span with one client. When the client was finally ready to order equipment for the project, they bought it from Jacob's competitor. It devastated him. Jacob had excellent excuses: Their prices weren't competitive, the competitor was a close friend of theirs and went fishing with them every year, and he needed more time to connect with them. Jacob's boss wondered if he had what it took to succeed.

I had the employer provide Jacob a DISC behavioral assessment. The results shocked the employer. It turned out that Jacob was very much an introvert with a high inclination toward details. In the original interview with him and most interactions, he seemed outgoing and personable. But once he had the report, his reluctance to want to visit clients, and wanting to spend a lot of time preparing for those meetings was making more sense.

There were other aspects of the report that helped pinpoint where Jacob's strengths and weaknesses lay–which gave us a lot to work with. The report confirmed Jacob was well-suited as a commission salesperson–he just needed to be calling on the right clients in the right atmosphere.

> The comprehensive DISC report impresses clients, and most agree it's ninety-five percent accurate. It bases the results on observable behavior, so the results are not a surprise to others that know the individual.

Jacob poured over every detail of the report and agreed that the report was accurate. There were recommendations on how to best communicate with him and where his strengths and weaknesses lay. It also pointed out that one of his strongest driving forces was resourcefulness, which is critical for a commission salesperson. A desire to succeed drove him. He wanted his actions to provide a return on investment. He was interested in financial rewards.

Based on his introverted style, the executive team expected Jacob would procrastinate making phone calls. Was there a way to force Jacob to make calls or visit his clients? Their two largest engineering clients had many meeting rooms and large lunchrooms, so they suggested Jacob work in one of their offices on Tuesday, and another client's office on Thursday. He was to be there all day.

Jacob was not pleased with this change of events. It frustrated him. "I'm supposed to sit in their lunchroom all day? What if someone asks me what I'm doing there, not meeting with anyone?"

"Tell them we recognize they're a very important client," his boss said, expecting his likely disapproval. "We recognize they are the largest mechanical engineering company in the city, so we want to be more available for them. Make it sound like we're adding more value and we wanted to start this special service with their firm. See what they say."

Jacob was fuming. Our client thought he might quit, but they were at their wits' end.

"Ok." He sat upright and half-demanded, "I won't be coming into the office those days then. I will travel directly to their offices and then home from there."

"Sounds fine." The client was happy to give almost any concession.

THE FOLLOWING WEEK, he went to both clients' offices. It started off a bit awkwardly. Slowly, word got out in the office that a competent mechanical engineer, who was also a nice, personable guy, was sitting in their lunchroom, ready to help. You could expect him every Tuesday.

One by one, these introverted engineers would poke their heads around the corner and ask Jacob to review projects with them. It wasn't long before the clients got used to having Jacob there and loved being able to just drop in on him. He selected some very complicated custom Air Handling Units, offering some fantastic advice and precision selections. He could provide a drawn-to-scale AutoCAD drawing they could insert into their project drawings. His understanding of fan and heat exchanger selections were impressive. Soon he had a lineup.

Amazing things happen when strength meets strength.

Jacob worked from his strength, rather than struggling through his weakness, and became a success story. It wasn't all to do with matching his style to his customer. Jacob is a smart man, a hard worker, and has charisma. But by increasing his odds of success, those attributes compounded his appeal.

Takeaways

- Use your DISC knowledge. Knowing is not enough.
- Use cheat sheets to keep the characteristics of each style nearby
- Be mindful that you likely have blind-spots, related to your DISC style. Ask a trusted adviser to help you improve these.

ESTABLISH YOUR BASELINE. PROCRASTINATE WITH INTENTION

"*Once we accept our limits, we go beyond them.*" Albert Einstein.

WE ARE all self-conscious about our limitations. We may say we intend to improve that flaw one day, but that day rarely arrives. Instead, we go through life wondering if we could have overcome our weaknesses.

And you know what? That is perfectly OK. It makes us unique. The trick is how to accept our mediocrity. Especially when we seem to have more than our fair share of limitations.

ONE DAY, a friend commented on my ignorance regarding the mechanics of an automobile. As an engineer, I felt I really should know more. The comment stung. However, it didn't sting badly enough to want to learn more. I just felt bad.

A month later, it happened again. This time, it stung a little more. Reluctantly, I decided I needed to do something about it.

I ran the issue through ABC1. I wasn't angry (A), but I was a little embarrassed. Next, I needed to figure who I was blaming.

That was easy. I was blaming myself. I really should know more about cars. My brother did all his own car maintenance from the day he learned to drive. Two of my brothers-in-law own collector cars, and also were confident to tinker under the hood. I would never know what they know.

But where to start? How could I take control? Did this mean every time I was embarrassed, I had to learn something? This seemed like a massive chore, and it would mean regularly working on things that didn't interest me. Plus, I had no time to do any of this.

How could I Control this situation?

I KNEW I could control the amount of blame I put on myself and could give myself the benefit of the doubt. That was a good start. My intent was good. I just didn't want to learn about cars. Did I have to? No. Why didn't I? Because I was busy working on things more important to me. OK. So could I forgive myself not knowing about cars? In the future, if someone makes a comment about my lack of knowledge, would I be OK with it?

This whole process was uncomfortable, but I ended up with, "I like nice cars. I just never cared enough to get into the working details of them. I've invested my time becoming an expert in other things and enjoy sport-related hobbies instead."

That resonated with me. It was true. And with that, I no longer concerned myself with car mechanics. Case closed. Inadequacy accepted. This may sound simplistic, self-absorbed, and unnecessary. But it truly provided me with relief. So much so, it encouraged me to contemplate other inadequacies. I know. Fun, right?

We don't have to be happy about our limitations, but we

need to either accept them or plan to change them. This is how we set our baseline.

"You can't go back and change the beginning, but you can start where you are and change the ending." C. S. Lewis.

I took C. S. Lewis's advice and planned to change some "endings" in my life. I picked the most important ones and set the rest aside. As you accept the past and make plans for your future, you bulletproof your mindset.

Time to take inventory:

If you are not actively improving your finances, fitness, health, career or your Frisbee toss, then you need to be OK with where you are at this moment. You cannot change it at this moment.

If your Frisbee toss is not that great today, and you're not working on it, then it's OK. Imagine how good your toss could be if you took a lesson from someone and practiced with them for a week. You could be a star! But who has time for that! The answer is, we all do. We just choose not to spend our time in that category of life.

If you don't have a plan to improve your financial status, then you may as well be OK with where you are. Financial status is one aspect where we all have a gauge of how we are doing. Most of us believe we should be doing better.

When you decide you are no longer OK with your finances, then you will need to take stock and set a goal for how you're going to get better. Even if you pick a small improvement, you will feel better immediately. One step is to start tracking your finances into a home finance software program, such as

Quicken. Taking even that one small step can make you feel more in control of your life.

You can be OK with your current status, and dissatisfied. Use that dissatisfaction to improve your top priorities. And the best way to do that is by working on that one thing. Not everything.

Here is a list of categories to keep in mind while you are contemplating this strategy.

- Personal Finances, retirement ready, and Net Worth.
- Personal Fitness, nutrition, weight, health.
- Career - future. Am I on a worthwhile career path?
- Social life. Friends, activities, hobbies.
- Learning. Reading technical literature, online lectures/seminars, courses, education, current events, politics, history, learning software. Do I feel my knowledge is increasing at a good rate?
- Personal Life and Family. Spouse, kids, parents, vacation. Is my work/life balance in balance?
- Spiritual life.

* * *

A true story.

Emily Cablek believed in her heart she would see her children again, and when that day came, she needed Child Services to grant her custody. Her ex-husband had abducted her 5- and 7-year-old children and gone into hiding three years previously. She struggled with depression and anxiety, blaming herself for everything that had happened, even when it was clearly not her fault. She was completely consumed with her grief and losing the children.

If the children resurfaced now, Child Services could interpret her anxiety and stress as being unfit for custody. Without knowing if the children were alive, she took control of her life through in-depth counseling. She had a goal to be ready for her children. She decided to have hope for her future.

When her children resurfaced in Mexico a year later, her twelve months of preparation were invaluable. Through her training, she knew her first reunion meeting would be more about the children than about her. The children had been through a lot. They were moving back to a country whose language differed from the Spanish they had been speaking for the last four years. She could not be overly emotional in her first meeting with them. She had to be the strong one for the children once they reunited. When that moment arrived, she was prepared and strong..., and she regained custody. *Piya Chattopadhyay, "Together Again," Out in the Open. CBC Radio One, Winnipeg, Canada, October 18, 2019.*

LIKE EMILY, you are standing at the birth of your future today. Whether you are feeling hopeful or hopeless, resist the temptation to take on too much.

* * *

IF YOU COMPLETE one goal in ninety days, would you be happy? If you could exercise one more time per week, would that feel good? Picture yourself having already accomplished that goal ninety days later. How do you feel having worked out more times in the last ninety days than you have in the last year?

We are going to go through an exercise. To prepare for that, take two minutes and decide which aspects of your life you are happiest and where you need the least amount of improvement. Give yourself some credit for what you have accomplished. Give yourself gratitude for the person you've become. If you are happy with your physical fitness, give yourself credit. Give yourself credit for having a solid career, or a good social life, or good family. Wherever things are good, make a note and revel in that feeling for a few seconds. No matter how small, give yourself some credit.

NOW THINK through those aspects of your life where you know it could be better. But cut yourself some slack. Feeling bad will change nothing. Remember, you can't change any of this at this moment. You are where you are. This sounds so simple, yet in practice it is difficult to do because we feel like we should be better in so many ways.

If we accept our uninspiring financial status as it is today, does that mean we have failed? We thought we would be so much further ahead at this point in our lives. Admitting our mediocrity can be painful. Admitting we aren't where we thought we should be at this point requires vulnerability.

We must first accept the good, the bad, and the mediocre. Use this point as a launching pad to achieve great things. The difference is you are going to have a plan this time.

The same goes for your business baseline. Acknowledge if it will benefit the entire operation. But don't take the easy road of only doing what you are best at. If your finance needs fixing, start fixing it, even in the smallest way.

* * *

EXERCISE:
Add another layer to Bulletproof your Mindset.
Setting up a baseline and establishing goals requires effort

and perseverance. I'm providing you the full exercise to complete, but even completing a portion of it will make you more bulletproof. This section requires putting pen to paper and will provide concrete outcomes. You may wish to do this now, or you may decide to come back to it once you've implemented the other bulletproof strategies. Either way, it will still be here when you return.

STEP 1: Procrastinate with intention.

Pick a goal you want to accomplish, but you will not work on it for at least a year. Any goal is fine. At this point, you want to get in the habit of putting at least one goal on the shelf. Maybe it's something you've been meaning to do and haven't been able to get to. Make it official. Put that goal off for a year. Make procrastination work for you!

I gave up swimming for a year. It is on my longer-term horizon, as it is an excellent exercise for the entire body. I've heard you can reach a Zen-like state once you get in the groove. Once I can devote myself enough time to develop better technique, I will take it up again.

Another goal I'm putting off is learning a software program I use at work. I know it will help me, but it is a big commitment I need to set aside for now.

This exercise should be fairly easy for you to do. Do this right now. Pick one thing and write it down.

STEP 2: More procrastination with intention.

Now pick at least one goal you won't work on for three to five years. I gave up playing the piano for three years–maybe longer, but not so long that I'd sell my piano. I prefer to play guitar in my spare time. I picked the one I can enjoy with friends. I love playing piano, and it doesn't take up much space. Perhaps something will change down the road.

Since I have set that goal aside, I am no longer bothered if someone asks if I play piano. I used to feel bad I couldn't bang out a few songs. Now I don't. I play once every few months, and that's OK. That is just one small thing, but magnify it by multiple goals, and you will feel yourself becoming more bulletproof with every goal you can put off for at least a year.

Another goal I set aside was to buy a commercial building. The business required our full attention at the time, and drawing this into our priorities would be too big a distraction.

IDENTIFY how the goal fits into your overall plan or dismiss it entirely. I kept the piano goal, but I've given up the possibility that I will understand auto mechanics (although I recently changed my first flat tire!) Write the goals you won't work on in your One Year and 3-5 Year lists. Put at least one in each category. If you can put more in these categories, that's even better.

STEP 3: Where do you want to improve?

Review your baseline and seven life categories. (You could use the daily, fifteen-minute habit from Chapter 3 to work through this exercise.)

Keep your "won't do" goals in mind as we touch on other aspects of your life. (The following will take three to five minutes.) Think about where you stand in each of the seven categories mentioned earlier for thirty seconds each. Summarize where you want to improve, and give yourself a rating out of ten, ten not requiring any improvement. It's just a quick overview.

. . .

Step 4: List all goals you would still like to accomplish.

Write a quick, ideal goal list, using those categories as placeholders. List goals in each of these categories—whatever comes to mind is fine at this point. Write without editing for four minutes and don't worry if the goals are crystal clear. We will discuss SMART goal setting in the following chapter. It's just a brainstorming exercise at this point. If you accomplish one or two of these goals, you would be happy. That means it would be OK, or normal, if you did not accomplish any of these goals. You can pick simple or complex longer-term goals. Go ahead.

Step 5: Decide which goals can wait for 90 days.

Circle those items. When you commit to this "Not yet" list, you will feel a sense of relief, and you will create space to work on those things most important to you. If you're sitting on the fence whether you are going to work on an item, defer it to later.

Pick those things you don't have to do for three months or longer. Maybe it is fitness or nutrition or your spiritual life. Perhaps you will put off going back to school or learning a new musical instrument. Remember, it is not forever, just for at least three months. The wonderful news is, as opposed to setting goals, you don't have to have a detailed plan about not doing something! So, this part should be easy.

Step 6: Pick the one thing you will work on.

Pick one thing to do in the next 90 days. You may believe you could easily handle two goals, and that's possible. However, I only want you to have one primary goal. You can work on the other thing, but it's not your primary goal. When you have to decide which thing you're going to work on, your number one goal will always win that choice. When you know what your most important task is, like a laser beam, you become bulletproof. If you know what tasks you won't do, you can ignore those.

For example, if anyone asks you to go golfing, you can say, "I've given up golf for now, because I want to spend more time with my family, and no one in my family golfs. I go biking and hiking with them instead. I find the fitness component to be much more satisfying." Combining what you won't do, and your most important goal, fuels your bulletproof nature.

My primary goal was to finish my first draft for this book. I was told how difficult it would be. I knew it would require my full focus. I had several other interests keeping me busy, including my consulting/coaching business, and getting my BusinessPartner4Hire.com website running. I kept those tasks active, but I focused on my writing goal with as few distractions as possible. When I sat at my desk, I knew task number one was writing. I didn't have to weigh which task I should do. It was always writing.

That doesn't mean I only wrote. I did other things that could help with other goals, but if I sat down and had to pick a task to complete, I could always start with writing, and that would be the right thing to do. When I didn't feel like writing, I would do research, or figure out what my next writing task was. When I got stuck, which would happen from time to time, I would lay out a plan, and start with the easiest task to pick up some momentum that would then get me doing the tougher part of writing.

WHEN YOU KNOW what your most important task is, you become bulletproof. If I had three goals, instead of one, the toughest goal of those three would not get done. I could reason I was achieving these other goals, so it was fine not to work on the tough goal. But the best goals are always the toughest goals. If you aren't working on your tough goal, then make every other goal secondary, or even set it aside until the tough one is complete.

DON'T USE victim language for why you are quitting something.

If you say you quit playing golf, because you just can't find the time, or your wife doesn't golf–you sound like a victim. It sounds like you're blaming your family or your job for stealing your free time. The language you use is important. Your brain will take your negative language and make you feel weak and victimized. This is not Bulletproof, and it makes you feel resentful.

If you are not working on your weight or nutrition, you can say, "No. I've put that off for three months while I'm rehabilitating my knee." Take responsibility for why you are dropping things off your list. Don't blame anyone.

EVERYTHING GOES on one of these three lists.

1. List of goals I'm <u>not</u> working on for at least the next twelve months–a lengthy list is fine.
2. The one or two goals I'm working on in the next ninety days. One is excellent. If you have two, pick one to be the top goal.
3. List things I might work on–once ninety days have passed. This is the list between 3 months and 12 months.

THESE LISTS ESTABLISH YOUR BASELINE.

Let's say you don't make this list, and someone asks you about the book you are writing. You make excuses about why you stopped writing, and that you're waiting until your career job is past its busy season. Regardless of your reason, you feel sheepish, and you disappoint the friend who asked you the question.

You make the same excuse with each person who asks you. You are discouraging one person after another with your lack of commitment and persistence. After a while, they grow accustomed to your lack of progress and stop asking. You sense their disappointment. Your negative vibe is rubbing off on you more than you think.

Instead, turn it around and make the three lists. You put off working on your book for the next six months while you are focusing on your fitness. You tell the next person about the progress you're making on your fitness plan! You are thirty days into it, and you've already lost a few pounds, and you're running in your first five-mile run in two weeks. You are excited about it and walk away feeling happy and proud! Every acquaintance gets the same story, and you feel your self-confidence grow. What a difference! All these minor things add up! Your focus is on your fitness. Not writing your book is no longer a failure—you have planned to set it aside.

Before we get into the important distinctions in setting goals, we need to consider what our limits are.

TAKEAWAYS:

- We all have our limitations. Acknowledge them and allow yourself to be OK with your mediocrity.
- Take an overall inventory of aspects of your life.

- Accept that you cannot change anything at this moment. Resolve to be OK with where you are.
- Resolve to work on that one thing. Not everything.
- Give yourself some gratitude for those areas in your life you are proud of, regardless of whether it has been easy for you.
- Decide you will delay working on a goal for a year. Procrastinate with intention.
- Delay all goals, except one.
- Make a clear plan to achieve that one goal.

MAKE FRIENDS THAT ARE REAL FRIENDS

Your relationships should empower you, not bring you down.

GIVE yourself fifteen seconds to think about that comment.

DID you think of a specific relationship where you always feel worse after being with them? Do you know why? It is normal not to know why. It's normal to feel uneasy about a relationship without being able to put your finger on it. But our instincts are trying to tell us something.

What do we want from our personal relationships? We want fun, positive people that encourage us and support us, especially through our tough times. We like people with similar hobbies and lifestyles. We like interesting friends who introduce us to new activities and enlighten us with their unique points of view.

The more you get to know someone, the more candid you become with each other. Eventually, the honeymoon will be over. You become less cautious with your comments. The curtain has fallen away. Now it's time to see if you are good friends.

* * *

In Grade 10, John, Dave, Danny and I hung out every day. We considered ourselves rebels, pushing the limits of our teenage environment. John considered himself as the king rebel. If we didn't follow his ideas, we were wimps.

He didn't like organized groups and thought school sports were for losers. At the time, I was seriously considering playing basketball and football.

One day I had enough. I don't remember what he said, but I was done. I told Danny, "There's something about John and Dave that I don't like, and I don't see it getting any better. I don't know who I will hang around with, but it's not them." We were only fifteen years old, but it left a scar. I ended up joining the football and basketball teams and met friends who were more positive.

* * *

Breaking up a bad relationship, even when it's clearly the right thing to do, can still hurt. It's a combination of remembering the good times, along with the shame that you were the friend of this person. In retrospect, I had probably outgrown John, who wasn't open to other's ideas. He wanted to keep our small band together, and I wanted to meet other people and expand my horizons. I was initially attracted to his rebel way of thinking. Eventually, I grew tired of it.

. . .

We have our greatest mindset growth in our early twenties. We are exposed to so many new ideas, it's easy to get engrossed in an area that other friends have no interest in.

As a result, we outgrow people around us. Some catch up, some never do. They are comfortable with where they are, or so afraid of change, that they stay stuck in their world forever.

Accept that some relationships are not fixable. Don't hold grudges.

We grow when we apologize sincerely. We may want an apology in return, or an acknowledgment they contributed to the poor state of our relationship. We may want them to, at least, accept our apology. None of these may happen. You can do everything on your end, but if the other person doesn't want to see your side of the story, then you need to take responsibility for that outcome.

Deciding that a relationship no longer serves you can be liberating. You don't have a choice, anyway. Your other choice is to stay upset about it, which serves no one, especially you.

Decide you did what you could and come to a conclusion. Stop beating yourself up. Then burn that decision in your mind so you can recall it when you relive that relationship. Because you will relive it. Over and over. Don't make a new decision about how you feel each time you run the relationship through your head. Stop torturing yourself over relationship issues that will never resolve themselves. Forgive yourself. Forgive offenses against you. Take full responsibility. Don't hold grudges.

One of my favorite quotes of all time is from author and renowned speaker Jim Rohn, *"What you have at the moment, you've attracted by the person you've become."*

. . .

I READ this early in my career. I interpreted it to mean, the better I become, the more money I will make, and the more stuff I can buy. Money was a great thing to focus on when I was younger, because it seemed to be within my grasp.

When I returned to it years later, I realized it applies to so much more. We've attracted our career, our finances, our personal growth, our family relationships, and our friendships. And none of it was luck. We did it to ourselves, and our friends are key to all of it.

We have attracted our friends by the person we've become. If we are positive, ambitious, and open to meeting new friends, we are more likely to meet people like that. But... we may have to leave our comfort zone to meet those people.

Meeting the right people

Early in my career, my friends were positive, but they weren't driven to succeed at business. I wanted to meet people like that. Jim Rohn said I first had to become the person I wanted to meet. It's hard enough to make friends, and now I have to find positive, ambitious friends? Won't they already have too many friends? Where would I find these people? I needed to put myself out there–volunteering, or networking events, or in self-improvement seminars. Ugh. It was going to be uncomfortable.

I started by attending a local Board of Trade meeting. My boss suggested I go. Open yourself to opportunity, he said. After attending a few meetings, a director of the Board encouraged me to volunteer for the Civic Affairs committee. I remember thinking to myself; I do not know what civic affairs are. This must be the committee no one else wants. I hope no one asks me anything.

Turned out that Civic Affairs simply encouraged communication between the Board and the city, regarding land and building use, planning and development, and other community issues. I wasn't able to contribute much early on, but it was interesting. Six months later, I could say hello to a dozen people at the meetings. Not so bad.

Around that time, I met Geoff, a lawyer, and Peter, a stockbroker. Both were just getting started in their careers, similar to me, and I could sense a positive vibe from both of them. The three of us hit it off. Geoff invited me to his Toastmasters International group, which met on Tuesday evenings. Peter knew the local Junior Achievement (JA) group needed someone with a sales background.

Two weeks later, I joined both Toastmasters and JA and made friends in both organizations. I was already playing basketball and hockey twice per week, so my schedule filled up. No time to get together with my less ambitious friends...

DALE CARNEGIE LAID out how to connect with people and make a good impression in *How to Win Friends and Influence People.* He said, "You can make more friends in two months by becoming interested in other people than you can in two years by trying to get other people interested in you."

If you want to make friends, put that quote on your fridge. It's so simple to say, yet so difficult to do, unless you plan to do it. Yes, in the beginning, many of us need to plan to be interested in someone. Others have this skill built-in, but they are the minority. The rest of us are much more interested in ourselves.

HERE IS a line of thinking that has helped me: If you want to make a friend, be a friend. If you want someone to like you, like them first. If you want someone to trust you, trust them first. If you want others to find you interesting, be genuinely interested in what they are saying. You reap what you sow. You get what you give away. Remember that when you want something. Do you want to make more money? Yes. Are you suggesting I give away money first? Maybe!

First step: Stop thinking about yourself! Second step, what could you give away? Ask some questions: Who will give you the money? Your boss? And what does your boss want, and why would they give you more money?

Here is where you can give something in advance. Give them more value. Prove you are worth more, or promise to do more. Or, ask what you can do to earn more. If the boss says you can't earn more, then it's time to find a career where you can.

If you want someone to buy your product, think first about what they want. What does your product or service do that satisfies their want? Do you know what they want for certain? Ask them. What is it about my product that is most important to you? You'll think it's price, but an honest buyer will tell you it's not, most of the time.

IF YOU WANT to take responsibility for making new friends, then here is your chance. Allow yourself to step out of your comfort zone and meet your best friends. The more effort you make, the better the quality of friend. Take a chance. Strike up a conversation. Ask someone to meet you for coffee or lunch. This is how it starts. Most of the time, the person you meet is open to making new friends.

> One of least invasive ways to break the ice is with the acronym FORD. Family, Occupation, Recreation and Dreams. If you are at a work event, then occupation questions are easy. If you are at a personal event, then family and recreation have a natural fit. Dreams can fit in once you've had the conversation going for a little while.

By asking a question, the other person does the talking. And then follow Dale Carnegie's advice and be genuinely interested in the other person's reply. Sometimes, the right question can stimulate a fifteen-minute conversation. If you practice this, it will amaze you at how often people are happy to talk with you. Practice everywhere. You will find friends in the oddest of places.

If this feels disingenuous to have to remember to be interested in someone, try it a couple of times before you dismiss it. The results will surprise you.

Most people want to talk about themselves. They can hardly wait for someone to finish their story so they can tell their own story. And while they're waiting for you to finish, they are formulating their response and not listening to you. We know this happens. We see it every day. If you become the person who draws out other people, and becomes genuinely interested in them, you will be in the minority, and welcome at any gathering.

* * *

MASTERMIND GROUP

My Board of Trade friends Geoff and Peter and I started hanging around more often. It took six months before one of us suggested we form our own Mastermind group. It's a concept laid out by Napoleon Hill in his book *Think and Grow Rich*. A Mastermind group has like-minded peers who meet regularly to share ideas. In our case, we wanted ambitious people who wanted to grow their personal and professional development. We decided we would meet every week.

Our format was to have one of us share a concept from a book we were reading. The balance of the meeting was checking in with each other's goals and holding each other accountable. It was invigorating to listen to peers who wanted to grow–developing positive attitudes to improve our lives.

It worked very well, although we didn't always succeed. We each struggled from time to time with our goals, but we helped each other get back on track. Those sessions where someone needed extra encouragement were the best.

AFTER THREE MONTHS, we decided we should spend a longer session on the weekend where we could map out our goals. We still talk about that special day. We pushed ourselves to our limits.

Any goal we made had to be SMART: Specific, Measurable, Achievable, Realistic and Time-oriented. We challenged each other's goals, and how they would achieve them. What an amazing day. (More about that experience, and SMART goals in the next chapter.)

YOU COULD SAY you don't have anyone to have a Mastermind group with, or don't know how to form one. Hopefully that frustrates you. So now, take responsibility and take control of the situation. Don't give up so easily. Mastermind group information is everywhere. You can read the book, borrow it at your library, and start talking about a mastermind group. You will attract others, I guarantee it.

You may not attract the perfect group to start, but you will find one person. Maybe the two of you can find other strong people. One step at a time. Then follow the simple suggestions of the Mastermind group and watch great things happen.

. . .

STRONG FRIENDSHIPS ARE an important layer to Bulletproof your Mindset. Start by taking more control of just one relationship. Transition it to a more positive experience.

I want you to apply ABC1 with one of them. Pick the friendship that frustrates you the most. You don't need to know why you're aggravated. It may be a simple annoyance, or it may be something more complex.

* * *

TAKEAWAYS:

- Do something about that relationship that doesn't serve you.
- You attract your friends by who you've become.
- Forgive. Don't hold grudges.
- Meet the right people by being where those people go to meet new friends.
- Become genuinely interested in other people.
- The best conversationalist is the one who listens the most and draws out others.
- Start a mastermind group, even if it's just two of you to start.

SMART GOALS, AFFIRMATIONS AND VISUALIZATIONS

"*Do just once what others say you can't do, and you will never pay attention to their limitations again.*" James Cook.

PETER, Geoff and my experience on our goal-setting day felt overly ambitious. Sure, we knew we should set goals, but this seemed almost too much.

Peter was very prepared, arriving with ten pages of handwritten notes. He was ready! I remember thinking to myself, wow; I think he may have gone too far. Geoff's goals were more in line with mine–ambitious, but not impossible.

As we got started, you could feel the energy growing in the room. Endless possibility and potential surrounded us. We went through a few pots of coffee, nailing down intermediate steps to ensure we would remain on target, setting dates for us to hold each other accountable. It was an exciting, mentally exhausting five-hour session. We challenged and encouraged each other with every step.

Once we were satisfied with our plans, we closed our notebooks and had a few beers to unwind. It was a combination of relief and exhilaration. Being able to work together helped us feel we could actually accomplish the goals we had just set.

PETER AND GEOFF have achieved major accomplishments in their business and personal lives. When I reminisce about our threesome, it's not that we set goals, but how we did it. Reaching goals requires planning, uncommon persistence, and experiencing self-doubt along the way. Having like-minded cheerleaders holding each other accountable for that critical period in our lives was priceless. Together we grew to new levels from that day forward. Our seemingly unattainable goals became workable.

KNOWING you can set a goal and achieve it is a key strategy to Bulletproof your Mindset. Billionaire H. L. Hunt said, "*First decide exactly what you want in life. Second, determine the price you will pay to achieve those things and third, resolve to pay that price.*"
If you don't give up anything, or plan to pay a specific price for achieving a goal, your likelihood of achieving it diminishes. Give up specific time wasters like TV and social media–even a small portion of that time. It will provide an immediate vacuum you can fill with goal achieving activities. Even if that goal is a fun activity or hobby, like playing guitar! Set a specific day or time to do your activity, and you'll automatically find yourself the time to do it.
Setting goals will enhance your mental toughness. I've set goals for most of my adult life. When I don't have goals, I feel something is missing. When I add goals to my life again, even if they are personal activities and hobbies, it improves my mindset. I've noticed people around me to be the same. When they

don't have an overall driving goal, they lose some of their zest for life. Without a challenge, we don't grow.

Look around you, and you'll find many goals whose outcome you can control. Having a balanced set of goals is important, including having a health and fitness goal. Experiment setting diverse goals and you will find one that resonates with you.

As you set realistic, achievable goals, you will feel a burst of energy. Your sense of urgency is ramping up. When someone is holding you accountable for a goal, your subconscious will encourage you. While watching television on a Wednesday night, you suddenly decide you should read the book you promised you would. We find time we never used before, when we have a goal we promise to reach.

* * *

Set a goal to practice Bulletproofing your Mindset.
Here is a list:

- Notice when you experience a negative emotion or are giving up. Be mindful when you feel agitated, frustrated, complaining, or angry. Jot yourself a note.
- Actively reduce your blame and notice if your anger reduces. Did it work? It should happen immediately. Note your successes and failures.
- Assume positive intent. How many positive intentions can you come up with for a specific situation?
- Look for areas where you can take responsibility where you haven't previously.

- Take control of the situation after you have reduced blame.
- Take control of the training for your career.
- Bring a positive outlook to your work.
- Develop a fifteen-minute habit to work on an important development project.
- Set a goal to find the friend you want to meet.
- Start or join a mastermind group.
- Take a DISC assessment.
- Use body language to guess someone else's DISC style.
- Identify someone with a DISC style opposite to yours
- Print off DISC quadrant cheat sheets.
- Establish your baseline.
- Take one goal and make it SMART.

Decide to set a SMART goal to develop one of the Bulletproof skills every three months. Making them measurable can take trial and error, but you will keep getting better at it.

ONE OF MY favorite methods for keeping track of goals is with a simple graph. Use dates along the bottom x-axis, and the eventual goal at the top of the graph y-axis. You draw a line from start date to finish date, and you have the daily work required.

The simple graph worked wonders for Geoff, who resolved to read a very tough, long, legal text on Corporate Business Law. Because of the dry, complicated nature of the text, he could only read twenty pages in one sitting. He made up a graph to get his reading accomplished (1800 pages). Three months later, he had slogged his way through it.

That was a proud moment for him, and the knowledge he gained in the process was invaluable. None of his peers had read that text from cover to cover.

"A JOURNEY of a thousand miles begins with a single step." Lao-Tzu, renowned Chinese philosopher

ONE OF MOST EFFECTIVE methods for achieving a goal is to ask to be held accountable. Kevin Armstrong, author of *The Miracle Manager: Why True Leaders Rarely Make Great Managers*, held me accountable for my first draft completion date for this book. He called me two days before my self-imposed deadline to find out if I would fulfill the promise I made to him. I was waiting for that phone call, and I responded with delight, "I am!"

* * *

MY FRIEND ROD read a book that tied rewards to achieving daily activities. Simple concept, but with two twists–a reward for completing a basic task, such as making a phone call to a prospect, could be as silly as dropping a paper clip into a cup or eating a smartie. The second twist was to check in with a partner at 5:00 pm every workday.

Rod and I each set three goals we had to accomplish one hundred percent–no wiggle room. My tasks were to make five quotation follow-up calls per day, to read a database programming book for fifteen minutes per day, and to set one appointment with a client per day. Our daily phone call lasted five minutes, with us reciting each item on our list. The concept encouraged activity-based goals, rather than selling a certain number of widgets or meeting a monthly sales target.

All tasks were achievable and ordinary for one day. But to string together consecutive days was where the challenge lay. That first week I scrambled to make my last phone call at 4:30 pm. Our conversation at 5:00 pm had us both smiling, acknowledging this would be no picnic. We hit our targets for the first five days. The calls resulted in a slight increase in sales, but uncovered opportunities that brightened the outlook for the next two to three weeks. It was energizing.

The second week was a little tougher, but we both stuck with it. We had made the easier calls in the first week. Week two would mean diving into more challenging client calls. By the end of that week, our sales took a jump. The sales funnel was growing, improving the outlook for weeks ahead.

In weeks three and four, the increased load processing new orders made it tougher to make those calls.

By the end of week six, our sales numbers were off the charts! We were both killing it. Our simple, important tasks had compounded, not unlike compound interest in your retirement savings account.

We continued with our check-ins, but we cut back on how many calls we needed to make. The momentum created a new animal that we needed to feed. Eventually, we stopped our experiment.

In that two-and-a-half months' period, my sales increased threefold. It was a year later before the effects wore off. It was difficult for us to admit this simple system could produce that level of success. Maybe we wanted to believe it was more us than the technique.

* * *

SMART GOALS

Once you've decided on a goal, you need to make it a SMART goal: Specific, Measurable, Achievable, Realistic and Time-oriented.

When someone asks you if you have achieved your goal, the answer should be a clear "Yes" or "No". Not "almost" or "90% done". Set your SMART goal so you can answer "Yes, it's done," or "No, it's not." For something so important, it's not asking too much to spend an extra ten minutes figuring out how to make a goal SMART.

When most of us first set goals, we unintentionally set them with wiggle room. We want to meet our goal, but we're not exactly sure how it's going to happen. We like wiggle room. It can help us save face.

Let's say I have a goal to run a marathon. What's missing in that statement? Time-Oriented is an obvious omission. So, let's set the date. My goal is to run a marathon by the end of 2022. That sounds better. Am I finished? Is any marathon good enough? When is my last chance in 2022 to run a marathon? If I only want to run the Vancouver Marathon, then the date is May 1, 2022. If I can travel to Portland, Oregon, then I have until October 4, 2022. Wow. That is a five-month difference! Good thing I checked now!

To make a goal measurable, the measure has to be specific. A marathon is already measurable as twenty-six miles, or forty-two kilometers. Do you have a goal to finish it under a time limit? Your training will be much different if you are trying to finish under four hours versus under five hours.

Achievable and Realistic often go together: Will your current health allow you to do this? Have you run a race before? This is where you will need to do your planning based on your current situation. When is the registration deadline? Are there any qualifications for that marathon? Is it too hilly for you? Is completion of four hours not realistic? For this one, maybe four and a half hours would be better.

We started with: I have a goal to run a marathon. We upgraded that to: "I am going to run in the Portland Marathon on October 4, 2022, and am going to finish in 4:30 or less. It is a popular marathon, and may sell out, so I will sign up now to be notified when registration begins. I have researched and found an eight-month training program that considers my current fitness level. I will begin that training on April 4, 2022."

I WILL UPDATE my website this year.

That goal has so much wiggle room it's ridiculous. It sounds OK, but it's terrible. It's not specific at all, is it? What updates are you going to do?

Instead, "I will update our Home page on our website and include at least two thirty-second videos. The company leadership team will approve the home page design by April 30, 2022. I will complete it by June 30, 2022." We've narrowed the amount of wiggle room, and we've added additional accountability to keep us focused mid-term.

Compare the versions of those goals. Initially, they feel vague and uninspiring–almost drudgery. The second, more focused goal feels exciting and energizes me to want to get started!

KNOW YOUR FIRST STEP.

You want to be crystal clear about your next step. If you walk away from a goal, and return a week later, and you aren't one hundred percent clear what to do next, then you haven't detailed out the goal enough. This is normal. Spend a little more time and get those first steps explicit. That way, when the kickoff day arrives, you won't need to think. Just action!

When I first asked my staff to set SMART goals, the percentage written SMART was twenty-five percent. One in four. I had explained the SMART process, but most still didn't get it right, and that's normal. I might not have explained it perfectly, or they may have been reluctant to ask questions.

Writing SMART goals improves with experience and getting it wrong a few times. You learn where you need to improve, and you do it again. Once you complete a tough SMART goal where someone has held you accountable, you will want to do it again. It's exhilarating.

As a small-business adviser, I encourage owners to have quarterly goals for all their employees. I teach them how important it is for the answer to be Yes or No, when they report at the end of the quarter. You want each employee to be judged the same way. It is done or not done. If you pat someone on the back for a goal that will be complete "next week", don't be surprised when next week turns into next month. Only reward one hundred percent completion. Done or not done.

It's OK to miss achieving a goal. In fact, you need to encourage yourself to set goals you may not achieve. It's how you Bulletproof your Mindset. The highest achievers set goals and regularly miss achieving them. People who fail and learn from that failure are bulletproof. They set a new goal, with a better plan to achieve it this time.

Thomas Edison, on failing 10,000 times to invent electric light, said, "*I have not failed, I've just found 10,000 ways that won't work.*" It takes uncommon persistence to achieve big goals—the ones that matter.

Affirmations are **key when you are stretching for a big goal.**

Rod also introduced me to the concept of affirmations. When you meet Rod and ask how he's doing, he'll say "Terrific!" with a big smile. You can count on that response, every time. Some days, you will know he's struggling to be genuine. But we know those positive words drive positivity into our subconscious.

Rod's encouragement led me to read the book *What to Say When You Talk to Yourself,* by Shad Helmstetter. The book contains many brilliant ideas and examples for positive self-talk.

As I read through the book, I tried an affirmation. I referred to it as "Handle paper once," also known as "single-handling." The simple premise is that if you open an email, or pick up a piece of paper, or take a phone call, you finish that task, either by writing it into your planner to work on later, or dealing with it now if you can finish it in five minutes.

When we are not single handling, we open an email, read it, then close the email. Why didn't you deal with it? Who knows? You didn't make a note, or anything else. You just knew you weren't ready to deal with it. When you go back into your email, and you see that email again, you scan your memory of why it's there. You open it up and read it again. You decide you aren't ready to deal with it. You close the email. Maybe you flag it. We open emails three or four times before we act on them. The really tough ones get opened ten times before we act on them. Or we finally delete them.

If you have a task on your desk, file it, write it on your list, and when you're ready to work on it, pull the file. The clutter and distraction of being surrounded with unfinished and unplanned tasks leads to terrible productivity–either finish it now or file it away. Sounds super simple and easy. It is not! It's one of the toughest things to maintain in a day. Add a phone call and meeting interruptions, and it is amazing we get anything done!

> Affirmations are the best technique for difficult to achieve habit changes. Shad Helmstetter advises injecting positive emotion into your affirmation and your chances of success increase significantly. Phrase your affirmations in positive language as if you have already achieved them.

My affirmation was, "I handle paper once and get tons of work done!" I repeated this out loud fifty times, three times per day. So, here I am, driving down the highway shouting and banging on my steering wheel, saying, "I handle paper once, and I get tons of work done!" Thank goodness the windows were closed. I tried to make it look like I was singing and playing air drums on my steering wheel if I noticed any weird stares from other drivers.

IT'S silly to think that we need to program our minds this way, but positive affirmations absolutely work. Your less ambitious friends may be very skeptical. That's OK. This is your secret power. Peter, Geoff, Rod and I all used them. The most successful business owners use them, as do the most successful athletes. Tiger Woods visualizes his putts rolling into the hole, then he pulls the trigger.

We use negative affirmations far too often. "I'm not good enough. I'm never going to finish this project. I can't lose weight. I don't enjoy exercising."

When you feel these negative thoughts enter your mind, turn them into a positive affirmation to counteract them. "I am at my ideal weight, and I feel and look great!" "I finish this project on time, and my boss congratulates me for a job well done!"

MY SINGLE HANDLING affirmation worked so well, it blew me away. My productivity went up at least thirty percent. If a task would take less than ten minutes, I would start and finish it. If I took a phone call and could respond in ten minutes, I would complete it. I completed simple product proposals in ten minutes and astounded my customers. They were accustomed to receiving proposals in two days, not ten minutes.

If I was in the middle of a longer task, I asked the receptionist to take phone messages. This seemed contrary to exemplary customer service, but she supported me once it was clear I would return phone calls when I said I would. (She was making promises on my behalf, so it was important that I kept my word and therefore, her word.)

Try single handling for a week. The first few days you will struggle with interruptions. But by the end of the week, you should notice a major change in your focus and effectiveness. Can you shut off all your notifications for thirty minutes–no buzzing, tweeting or ringing? If not single handling, pick a tough change you are trying to make. Emotionalize your affirmation, and say them three times per day, fifty times per session.

COMBINE AFFIRMATIONS WITH VISUALIZATIONS.

If you want to amplify your affirmations, combine them with visualizations.

I was a fan of affirmations, but I rarely used visualization, for no good reason. I know people that have had great success with it. After a few successes with affirmations, I wanted to try a risky SMART goal that had no wiggle room. This time, I included visualizations.

I DECIDED I would sell $50,000 worth of HVAC equipment in one week–not a small number, and not a huge number, but tough to achieve.

On my drive to work Monday morning, I was that guy banging on his steering wheel, saying over and over, "I sell $50,000 worth of equipment this week." I wrote $50,000 on some post-it notes and stuck them on my bathroom mirror, my workstation, and my computer screen. I wondered whether the spectacle I was creating would be worth the result.

Each day, morning, noon and night–I had my affirmation session lasting two or three minutes.

That week I secured two orders after 5:00 pm on Friday. Most contractor client hours were between 7 am to 4 pm, Monday to Friday. That week was different. I forget why it happened, but obviously it had something to do with my tenacity to achieve my sales goal. (My total number of orders I secured after 5:00 pm in the first ten years of my career? Two. Those two. So yes, this was a special week.)

In hindsight, I should have kept closer track of the orders I was getting, but I don't think I did because I thought I might fail.

AFTER I GOT the last order on Friday, I went to the primary order book that our receptionist Susan updated. I started writing out the numbers on a pink telephone message sheet: $4200, $76, $2356, $12,300, $587, $2900, $125, $610, $558, $2250, $8,800. Then I walked to the other order book in the far corner of the office. On the back of that same pink sheet, I wrote: $225, $800, $2100, $4475, $644, $3400, $1750, $390, $1100, $294. I totalled the front: $34,822 and totalled the back: $15,178. I was pleased with myself...

Alone in the office on a Friday evening, I totalled up front and back numbers and stared at this pink sheet.

5 0 0 0 0. To the dollar.

I FELT the hair on the back of my neck stand up. I totalled the numbers three more times. I sat there for at least ten minutes... Same total. OMG. My emotions were all over the place–happy, excited, proud, and scared.

I tried a technique to trick my subconscious into achieving something I wouldn't normally be able to achieve. To hit the number dead-on threw me for a loop.

I told some of my friends, and while it intrigued them, we didn't dive into it any deeper. To them, it was a cool story. To me, it felt like a message. Not necessarily a message from a higher power, but maybe a message from my self-conscious. "Anything you want to accomplish; you can do it. Just make a plan, set a specific goal, and go for it."

At the time, I justified it as an amazing coincidence. Today I know it was not a coincidence.

We all have so much untapped potential, it's staggering. And we know it. No matter what we have accomplished, we feel we could do more–achieve more, visit exotic locations on our beautiful planet, meet more people, and sample delectable food and drinks. The list goes on.

TAKEAWAYS:

- You can decide to achieve any goal you want. Resolve to pay the price to achieve that goal.
- Goals provide a zest for life, a drive that gives us energy and a positive sense of urgency.
- Set SMART goals to achieve Bulletproof skills.
- Set your critical goals as SMART.
- Missing a goal is a good thing. Recalibrate and set a new goal that you can hit.
- Use affirmations and visualizations to achieve your toughest goals.

EPILOGUE

I would love to know what my beliefs were twenty years ago.

During the research for this book, I was flipping through books that affected my life. I came across my handwritten notes inside *Tony Robbins' book, Awaken the Giant Within (1991)*, where Tony had provided two lined pages titled Empowering and Disempowering beliefs for readers to fill in. I was thirty years old, five years after I started practicing taking responsibility.

Here is what I wrote, verbatim:

My empowering beliefs were:

1. I do not allow myself to be controlled by anyone other than myself.
2. I control my feeling, my reality.
3. I am responsible for everything that happens to me.
4. If I work fifty-five hours per week, set goals on a

daily, weekly, monthly and yearly basis, I will be extremely successful.
5. If you do not work hard, you will not be successful.
6. It is when you work hard, when you don't feel like working, that you truly shown the difference between you and others.
7. You will be rewarded for the seeds you have sewn.
8. Happiness is not money. Happiness is friendships and contributions to others.

MY DISEMPOWERING BELIEFS WERE:

1. There does not seem to be enough time to do all the things I want to do.
2. It is hard to visualize being very wealthy.
3. I cannot turn my situation around quickly. It will be a three-year process.
4. We cannot afford a lot of things, including a cruise.

I REMEMBER how real those beliefs were for me. I had a chuckle about not being able to afford a cruise–not a car, or a house–but a cruise.

The first three empowering beliefs were all about taking responsibility, being responsible for everything that happens to me. I had drilled into my thinking that I controlled my reality. As I reread them today, I still feel one hundred percent committed to those beliefs. They are part of my reality twenty-five years later.

. . .

Here are my core beliefs today:

- I control my reality, which includes my attitude. The attitude I push out into the world returns to me.
- Most people mean well. Don't be upset with them. Instead, try to understand why they think and act as they do. We are all different and carry a heavy load.
- Most people believe they are working hard, but aren't doing the tough things required to become successful.
- Setting SMART goals is how you achieve the really tough goals.
- Success is a process. The greatest successes happen with persistence.
- Everyone can achieve a successful life - you just need to define your successful.

The disempowering beliefs I had written epitomized how frustrated I felt–skeptical about my future. Even having a firm belief in taking responsibility, I still had lingering complaints about time, wealth, and destiny. I wrote the beliefs like excuses. I was in a hurry to succeed, yet here were aspects of my life I wouldn't take responsibility for. At thirty years old, I felt like I had put in my time, and I was wondering why my rewards weren't showing up as I expected.

I wish I had notes from five years later.

EMBRACE YOUR BIGGEST FRUSTRATIONS. It means your biggest breakthroughs are around the corner.

It's when you won't give up, and keep pushing is when you achieve your greatest successes.

ABOUT THE AUTHOR

Paul is a small business adviser and entrepreneur. His passion is helping people realize their full potential, and helping their businesses do the same.

What he brings to the table is unique: An entrepreneurial, business owner, sales, construction, and engineering viewpoint on getting your business to the next level. More can be found at www.businesspartner4hire.com or www.paulaucoin.com. (Paul provides a limited number of adviser appointments that can be booked on these websites.)

Paul started HVAC Systems and Solutions Ltd. in 1999 in the basement of his house and grew it to $15M in sales and 23 employees before selling it in 2015. He had a 13-year Sales Engineering career with The Trane Company in Halifax, Sudbury and Vancouver before starting his own HVAC rep firm in Vancouver.

Paul is a founder of SHARC Energy Systems (CSE: SHRC). He provided his sales and technical expertise during startup of this wastewater energy saving technology.

He is a 14-year veteran of The Alternative Board (TAB). He learned that core issues in small businesses are the same, whether it's a trucking company, a consulting business a bowling alley business, or an HVAC Custom Equipment Supplier.

Some of Paul's greatest skills are helping implement sales strategies, implement key business processes as well as being certified in many of TTI's core assessments, including DISC, Driving Forces, EQ and TriMetrix HD. He has achieved Competent Toastmasters designation.

Paul and Ingrid have been happily married for 29 years and enjoy traveling and golfing together. Paul sings and plays guitar and is looking forward to jamming again with Shawn.

linkedin.com/in/paul-c-aucoin-18b1231a
twitter.com/BizPartner4hire
instagram.com/aucoin.paul

www.ingramcontent.com/pod-product-compliance
Lightning Source LLC
Chambersburg PA
CBHW070043120526
44589CB00035B/2293